AND ARE
WE YET
ALIVE?

AND ARE WE YET ALIVE?

The Future of The United Methodist Church

RICHARD B. WILKE

Abingdon Press / Nashville

AND ARE WE YET ALIVE?

Library of Congress Cataloging-in-Publication Data

WILKE, RICHARD B., 1930–
  And are we yet alive?
  1. United Methodist Church (U.S.)
  2. Methodist Church. I. Title.

BX8382.2.W55   1986   287´.6   86-3493

ISBN 0-687-01380-1

All Scripture quotations are from the Good News Bible, the Bible in
Today's English Version. Copyright © American Bible Society, 1976.
Used by permission.
  The Intensive Care Unit described in the letter on p. 76 is based on a
concept developed by J. David Stone in *Spiritual Growth in Youth
Ministry.*

MANUFACTURED BY THE PARTHENON PRESS AT
NASHVILLE, TENNESSEE, UNITED STATES OF AMERICA

To
the Church
I love and serve.

CONTENTS

SICK UNTO DEATH

Our sickness is more serious than we at first suspected. We are in trouble, you and I, and our United Methodist Church. We thought we were just drifting, like a sailboat on a dreamy day. Instead, we are wasting away like a leukemia victim when the blood transfusions no longer work.

Once we were a Wesleyan revival, full of enthusiasm, fired by the Spirit, running the race set before us like a sprinter trying to win the prize. The world was our parish; we were determined to "publish the glad tidings in the full light of sun." Our Wesley-inspired dream and directive was to "spread Scriptural holiness" across the continent. Circuit riders raced over hill and valley. New churches were established in every hamlet. Our missionaries encircled the globe.

Now we are tired, listless, fueled only by the nostalgia of former days, walking with a droop, eyes on the ground, discouraged, putting one foot ahead of the other like a tired old man who remembers, but who can no longer perform.

We sing "O For a Thousand Tongues to Sing" as if it were an anthem instead of a testimony. We celebrated bicentennial as if our future were behind us.

In addressing the Council of Bishops, I compared our

church in the United States to the paralyzed man, lying beside the pool near the Sheep Gate at Bethsaida. (John 5:1-15). He lay there, weak and withering away for thirty-eight years, surrounded by others who were blind, lame, and sick. Our denomination is now in its twenty-third year of diminishing strength, reclining close to the healing waters where the Spirit of God moves, yet remaining immobilized and infirm, waiting for someone to carry us into the waters of health.

The King James Version of the Bible says the man at Bethsaida was "impotent," meaning, I suppose, that he lacked the power to walk. But today, that seventeenth-century word *impotent* means unable to reproduce, and so we are.

Recently, I attended a large downtown civic luncheon. I was invited because our distinguished senior senator, Dale Bumpers, was the speaker. A member of our denomination, Senator Bumpers stood up and acknowledged that I, his bishop, was in the audience. That made me, and all the other United Methodists present, feel good. Then he proceeded to say that, like the blue whale and the great whooping crane, he was a member of an endangered species: He was a United Methodist. That made me and all the other United Methodists present feel bad, but he had spoken the truth. Since 1962, we have been lying by the pool, paralyzed, our power slipping away. We are unable to reproduce. We are a dying species.

The Facts

Once the subject for debate, the evidence now is fully documented. No longer can eternal optimists say, "Well, remember this" or "Don't forget that." The rose-colored glasses no longer protect us from the facts. Consider *church school attendance.* Years ago, one of our most able administrators, Bishop William C. Martin, accurately observed that there were many signs of alive congregations, but the one uniform signal, across the board, of a consistently alive, vibrant, and growing church was the strength of its church school attendance. During one period of great growth, the 1880s, 1890s, and early 1900s, the denomination had twice as many people attending the church schools as were members of the church. Children, youth, adults—visitors, friends, relatives—became a part of the church school and later made their commitment to the church.

Even as late as the 1950s and '60s the church school, by then less than the membership, was still the foundation for new members. Generally, about 70 to 80 percent of all persons received by profession of faith have come out of the church school. Church school attendance has been for us the gateway to Christ and the church.

The decline in our church school began in 1960 and has continued precipitously ever since. Prophets have cried out, "Look, look," because it is a "flag" statistic, but except for one brief, momentary pause in 1980, the plunge has continued unabated. Look at the figures in Chart #1 (p. 12).

These are not church membership statistics. Nor are they church school enrollment figures. They are not names on a roll in a dusty old book. They are the average attendance—live people with names like Martha and Sammy, Mr. Sullivan and Maude McKnight—in the church schools, dressed up on Sunday morning, present and accounted for, ready to sing "I Serve a Risen Savior." They are your sons and your daughters and friends of ours.

In 1960–1964—4.2 million

In 1980–1984—2.1 million

Half of our church school is gone! Over two million people are no longer with us. Those classes were, to use Lyle Schaller's phrase, "ports of entry" for our churches. Those people had "church growth eyes." They invited friends and neighbors to come with them to attend their classes. Eventually many experienced the living Christ in their lives and joined the church.

Warren Hartman of the General Board of Discipleship argues persuasively that the church school attendance figures are the first *predictors* of church membership change, leading the way by about two or three years. With

(Chart #1)

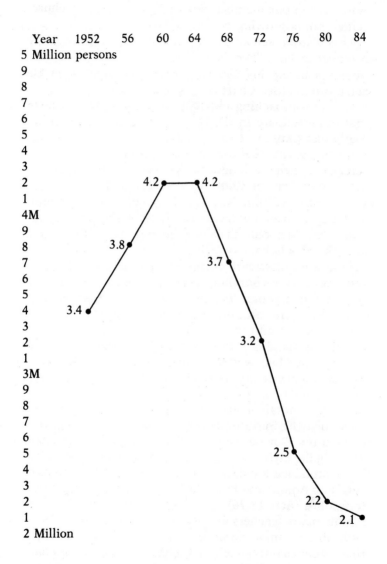

CHURCH SCHOOL
ATTENDANCE

| Year | 1952 | 56 | 60 | 64 | 68 | 72 | 76 | 80 | 84 |

5 Million persons

9
8
7
6
5
4
3
2   4.2 ●————● 4.2
1
4M
9
8   3.8 ●
7   3.7 ●
6
5
4 3.4 ●
3
2   3.2 ●
1
3M
9
8
7
6
5   2.5 ●
4
3
2   2.2 ●
1   2.1 ●
2 Million

Warren Hartman
GENERAL BOARD OF DISCIPLESHIP

church school attendance down by 1.8 percent for 1983 and 1.9 percent for 1984, it will now be three years before we can stop our membership decline even if the church school starts growing tomorrow.

The *church school enrollment* figures reinforce the attendance data. There is no hocus pocus, no playing with numbers here. This "bobsled" slides downhill over the same bumps (See Chart #2, p. 14).

We are approaching a loss of four million people who no longer participate in the church schools of The United Methodist Church. If these statistics had been gathered from a consumer sales company, somebody would have screamed "help" a long time ago.

Dr. Win Arn, of Church Growth Institute, makes a telling observation. Nearly 60 percent of our United Methodist churches have fewer than seventy-five enrolled in their church schools. Only 4 percent of our church schools have over four hundred enrolled, and 7 have one hundred fifty or more in attendance. The great number of our churches, four out of five, have small schools. In many parts of the country, that number is limited to children under twelve.

Do you remember your church school teachers? I remember mine. I believe I am in the ministry partly because of their powerful influence; they made an indelible mark on my life. For many of us, God used them as modern-day apostles. Like Barnabas, they were "sons [and daughters] of encouragement." Like Philip, who explained the Scriptures to the Ethiopian eunuch, they opened the Word of God to us—all the way from Jesus' blessing the little children, to the agony of Job's suffering. They explained the deep spiritual realities of life to us as surely as Aquila and Priscilla interpreted the Holy Spirit to Apollos (Acts 18:26).

How many teachers and workers did we have in 1964? 540,000. How many do we have now? 420,000. Where have these absent saints gone? To heaven, I think, and they have not been replaced. Once, the teacher training programs of the Methodists and the Evangelical United Brethren

(Chart #2)

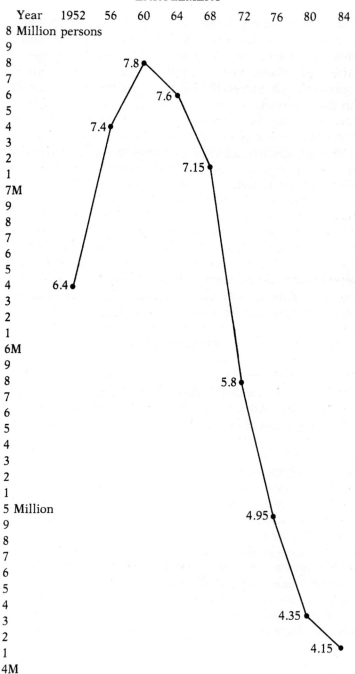

CHURCH SCHOOL
ENROLLMENT

Warren Hartman
GENERAL BOARD OF DISCIPLESHIP

(EUB) were shining lights, the benchmarks toward which other denominations would strive. Now, our workshops and lab schools are of good quality, but are modestly attended. Many pastors consider the teacher training opportunities, indeed the entire church school, irrelevant to their ministries. Many laymen and laywomen believe that teaching the faith is for someone else to do. Many churches do not spotlight the church school as the vital, essential, disciple-making and Christian nurturing program that it once was and can again be. Thousands of churches are allowing the church schools to grow older, as if only those over forty needed or wanted the experience. The truth is that the baby boom generation (ages 17–34) now has produced eighty million Americans. We are not reaching them. They are having children, the "baby boom-boom" generation. Our nurseries and preschools should be filled to capacity, but they are not. The baby boom generation and the generations to follow *need* the faith that we cherish and so loyally support.

Membership

So it is no wonder our membership declines. During the past few years, some voices have spoken out, pleading for attention to the draining of our life's blood. But often they have been drowned out by false prophets who cry "peace, peace, when there is no peace" (Jeremiah 6:14). Now the cry is a shout, and the whole church is asking the question: "What is happening to us—and why?"

The church membership figures have often been dramatically displayed. But to further sensitize ourselves to the situation, let's put this chart before us one more time. Now we can add 1984 because we have a net loss, and we will soon be able to add 1985, for the trend downward continues unabated (See Chart #3, p. 16).

John Wesley perceived a Methodist society's membership decline as a "sore evil" that needed remedy. Wesley argued that growth was a sign of God's grace, decline a sign of decrease in grace.

15

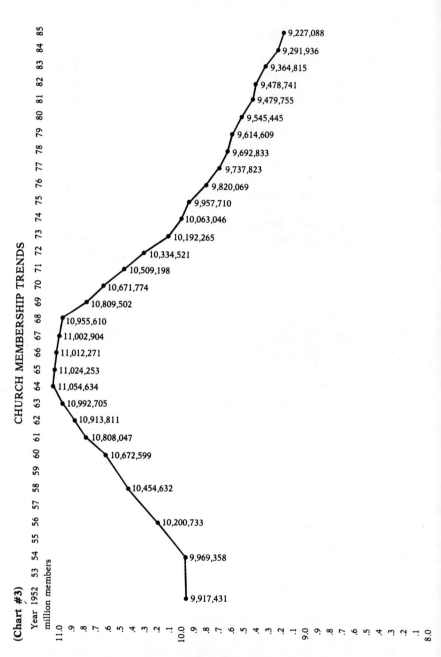

(Chart #3)

CHURCH MEMBERSHIP TRENDS

Year 1952 53 54 55 56 57 58 59 60 61 62 63 64 65 66 67 68 69 70 71 72 73 74 75 76 77 78 79 80 81 82 83 84 85

million members

9,917,431
9,969,358
10,200,733
10,454,632
10,672,599
10,808,047
10,913,811
10,992,705
11,054,634
11,024,253
11,012,271
11,002,904
10,955,610
10,809,502
10,671,774
10,509,198
10,334,521
10,192,265
10,063,046
9,957,710
9,820,069
9,737,823
9,692,833
9,614,609
9,545,445
9,479,755
9,478,741
9,364,815
9,291,936
9,227,088

Warren Hartman
GENERAL BOARD OF DISCIPLESHIP

I began speaking severally to the members of the society, and was well pleased to find so great a number of them much alive to God. One consequence of this is that the society is larger than it has been for several years. And no wonder, for, where the real power of God is, it naturally spreads wider and wider. (Journal 4/7/1760)

How Bad Is It *Really?*

What does this discouraging study of statistics mean? Some people say the situation isn't so bad as it seems. They argue that many congregations are vital and alive; millions of people are in worship; money keeps coming in; Third World United Methodist Churches are growing; many church rolls have been "cleaned"; numbers of people in other denominations are being drawn to our denomination.

I am convinced, however, that these arguments miss the point. They perpetuate illusions so that, even after more than two decades of unrelenting decline, we still refuse to face the harsh realities. Consider these myths:

Myth #1: *We have "bottomed out." Now we are ready to grow again.*

This argument was used after 1968. People insisted that the EUB–Methodist merger talks had required much energy—energy that would now be put into outreach ministry. But the merger brought no new evangelistic thrust. John Naisbitt says in his book, *Megatrends*, that the big business mergers have all the appearances of dinosaurs mating. Union between large denominations may be worthwhile, but it does not necessarily breed missional fervor.

Again, the argument was used in 1980 when, for the first time in nearly two decades, Sunday school attendance (a lead indicator) showed a momentary gain of a handful of people for that year. It was a grasping at straws; the attendance fell again the following year.

Finally, in 1984, the enthusiasm of the bicentennial caused many people, including myself, to believe that surely our excitement would generate new converts. That was froth on the ocean. In actuality, the many meetings—annual conferences, jurisdictional conferences, and general conferences—with the accompanying organizational and political activities, used up vast amounts of spiritual energy. The bicentennial activities were good for us, but they were clearly "within the family." During the bicentennial, we were like a retail business closed for inventory. No sales were made. Experts now tell us that General Conference years are typically the weak membership years in each quadrennium. Every time we have a General Conference we have a slump in professions of faith. The figures show a net loss in membership for 1984 with similar projections for 1985. The bicentennial did not turn us around.

Myth #2: *We are receiving many members by transfer, both from other United Methodist Churches, and from other denominations. We are receiving more from other denominations than we are losing to them.*

This gamesmanship glosses over the painful losses. Transfers among United Methodists are, of course, not growth factors at all, merely shuffling statistics within the fellowship. Worse, because some people are on two church rolls for a time, there is a lag, causing about twenty thousand people to be counted twice each year. It is true we are receiving more from other denominations than we are losing to those denominations, but our church is, for some of these people, a last hope, or at least a second chance. Then, if they become discouraged with us, they leave by withdrawal or conference action. The bottom line is still net loss.

Myth #3: *Whereas we had a million deaths between 1973 and 1983, we had fewer deaths in our denomination in 1984.*

That's right, but the argument is negative for two reasons. Because the denomination is smaller, fewer deaths are necessary to drain our community of faith as severely in terms of percentages as in earlier years. We now have a smaller church to die from. Warren Hartman's studies show that the death rate in our denomination climbed from 10.4/1000 in 1964 to 12.5/1000 in 1984. And the denomination is growing older. Many people are sick, shut in, and elderly. One key study shows that "mainline" denominations, including ours, are made up disproportionately of people over fifty years of age.

Myth #4: *We've been cleaning the rolls for twenty years, and now we're obtaining "hard figures."*

One bishop recently wished we could have a "jubilee year," when every church would clean its rolls once and for all. Then, he said, "we could start clear and fresh and begin to grow again."

However, we are losing people all the time. The rolls are not rigged; the weak retention rate bleeds us. If people still leave our churches "out the back door," we will have to clean our rolls year after year. Until we re-establish ways of nurturing our members, when they move about, grow up, have trouble, they will continue to leave us.

The Western Jurisdiction, for example, has the highest percentages of profession of faith additions, but it also has the highest percentage of charge conference deletions. How do we account for that? The answer is, I think: They have a small percentage of people in adult Sunday school classes. Apparently, the people are not intimately assimilated into the fellowship, so more than the average are eventually lost.

Myth #5: *We are part of a worldwide church. In many countries, the Methodists are growing.*

This statement is true, but watch out. The word *Methodist* is misleading. There are all sorts of Methodists: (a) other groups who have a Wesleyan heritage, (b) former Methodist conferences, such as the Korean Methodists, who have become independent, affiliate, or fraternal groups, and (c) actual Central Conferences of The United Methodist Church. These latter conferences are indeed part and parcel of The United Methodist Church, and most of them, especially in the Third World, are growing (noteworthy are Kenya, Zimbabwe, Sierra Leone, and the Philippines).

This overseas growth makes the total figures look encouraging, but overseas growth obscures the severity of the statistics in the United States. *Consider that in 1983 all annual conferences in the United States, except three, had a net loss in membership.* It is a good thing the Central Conferences overseas were growing.

Myth #6: *At least we are growing rapidly in the ethnic churches.*

Let's see. In the United States there is a large Hispanic population and a tremendous opportunity for ministry; the Spanish language television network (SIN) estimates a total of 22.2 million Hispanic people in the United States. We must agree with Naisbitt that it is becoming more and more obvious that every American should learn three languages—English, computer, and Spanish.

But what about our churches? Hispanic United Methodist members grew by 233 persons from 1974 to 1982. The Rio Grande and Puerto Rico Annual Conferences contain 73 percent of our Hispanic churches. These one hundred eighty Hispanic churches, over a five-year period, gained six persons, from 24,471 to 24,477. Church school enrollment dropped by eighty-three; total average worship attendance increased by thirty-seven, and church school attendance by the same number. In 1984, almost every church in the Rio Grande Conference showed a loss. Lyle Schaller writes, "Congregations in some areas of the country with the most rapid influx of Hispanic people have reported a loss in membership over the last five years, notably Chicago and Southern California." Yet, there has been some growth. Our current membership in Hispanic churches is about 37,500, which is a net gain over the past twelve years of about seven thousand people. However, most of that growth occurred about ten years ago and has now slowed down to a mere trickle.

One would think our emphasis on an inclusive church would be showing dramatic results, but a study by the General Board of Discipleship shows only five predominantly Anglo churches in Texas with as many as 10 percent Spanish surnames.

We have a strong black membership, showing modest increase in the midst of rapid population growth. In a General Board of Global Ministries study from 1974 to

1982, predominantly black churches grew by 2,265 members, or 1.3 percent. About one hundred forty churches were closed; very few new black congregations have been started in nearly twenty years. Inclusiveness is slowly strengthening. During those eight years, black participation in predominantly white churches increased by 2,265 persons.

Native American United Methodists decreased from 11,512 to 10,846, down about 4.9 percent. Participation in other churches decreased from 14,091 to 13,472, down about 4.4 percent.

Among Asian Americans the great increase primarily is among Koreans. They are growing in number of members, number of churches, and in participation in the total church life. Asian membership (in ethnic churches) jumped from 11,484 in 1974 to 26,153 in 1982, an increase of 127.7 percent. Over one hundred new congregations have been started. Participation in Anglo churches has more than doubled. The greatest potential for church growth among ethnic minorities in the United States right now lies with the Korean United Methodists.

These figures are significant, for the combined ethnic growth over eight years was 4.4 percent. During the same period, the entire church declined by 5.6 percent. Yet, without the Korean impact, growth would have been minimal. Ethnic inclusiveness has moved from 4.2 percent to 4.7 percent. (Source: Office of Research, National Program Division General Board of Global Ministries.)

One might ask, "Why hasn't the Ethnic Minority Local Church (EMLC) had a greater impact?" The answer lies here, I think: EMLC has helped empower ethnic peoples in the decision making structures of the church. EMLC has strengthened salary support, improved facilities, and highlighted severe racial injustices in our society. But the program has lifted some top leadership out of the local church. More important, our ethnic churches, even with this national emphasis, suffer from the same blight as the rest of the church, a failure in heart and mind of the ministry of the local congregation to make disciples.

Participation Down

Now, if some great wave of people were surrounding the formal membership of the church, waiting to enter, our deep fears for the future might be dispelled. But the contrary is true. Fewer youth are in our Sunday schools and youth fellowships each year. The number of children under the age of twelve in the Sunday school declined again last year, in spite of a new wave of babies born in our country. The United Methodist Women have fewer members, and most observers indicate that the organization is failing to reach young women. The United Methodist Men show organizational resurgence, because many new units have been formed during the 1980s. However, almost all units seem to be composed of very active laymen in the churches with few visitors or new converts.

Participation in full-time service holds steady in the ministry because of the significant surge of women, allowing us to hold our own in pastoral resources. In missionary work, however, the decline of missionaries from over sixteen hundred in the 1960s to about six hundred today has demoralized a generation of church men and women. Pastors today seldom challenge their people to give their lives in missionary service.

A leading Indonesian church member was asked whether the missionaries were needed in Indonesia. He replied that yes, they were. The people naturally don't want condescension nor do they need paternalism, but they desperately need fraternal workers, people who will work and witness alongside them and strengthen them in the hour when their country hinges on the balance.

The short-term missionary program (overseas for three years or within our country for two years, or US-2s) was a program that inspired President Kennedy to inaugurate the Peace Corps. Gradual decline in this short-term missional work has caused most pastors to become unconcerned. Our program has dwindled to twenty-eight US-2s in 1984.

New Churches Needed

Often we think of the rise or fall of existing congregations when we consider church membership or church school statistics. But integral to denominational growth or decline is the establishment of new churches. Historically, from the time of Paul's missionary journeys, new congregations have been planted in new population centers. Beginning fellowship groups glow with a new fire, often putting older congregations to shame. McDonald's hurries to each new town or urban development, raising the golden arches, in order to feed people billions of hamburgers. So, too, we must penetrate our complex culture with church spires to offer the bread of life to millions of people. This has been the strategy of the mission movement all over the world; John Wesley developed the "societies" throughout England, Wales, Scotland, Ireland, and splashed over into America.

William Warren Sweet, the "father of American church history," used to say that the Baptist farmer-preacher went right with the settlers, and the Methodist circuit riders were riding up to the log cabin before the roof was on. Those young preachers started new congregations, often by singing a passionate hymn, preaching a fiery sermon, and leaving behind a lay leader or class leader to hold together a congregation that soon became a church.

After the Civil War, a wave of people followed the advice of Horace Greeley to "Go west, young man, go west." Chaplain C. C. McCabe, assistant secretary of the Church Extension Society for the Methodist Episcopal Church, developed a dynamic strategy of church extension. From 1868 to 1884, he planted congregations across the country. One day, he noticed a newspaper article about Robert Ingersoll, the famous orator and agnostic. Ingersoll had proclaimed that "the churches are dying out all over the land; they are struck with death." C. C. McCabe leaped off the train at the next station and fired off a telegram to

Ingersoll. It read: "Dear Robert: All hail the power of Jesus' name—We are building more than one Methodist church for every day in the year, and propose to make it two a day!" (*The Story of Methodism*, Luccock)

Since the early 1960s we have been closing more churches than we have been opening—five or six times more! Dr. Lyle Schaller estimates that over four thousand of our EUB and Methodist churches have been closed since 1964. We have closed abandoned churches in rural areas where the population has practically disappeared. We have closed derelict church buildings in urban areas where the congregation has moved elsewhere. Instead of closing them, we should be revitalizing these churches with new forms of ministry. We should be constructing church buildings in new geographical areas. Severe population shifts are normal in our mobile American society, but the tragedy is that we have not been eager to go where the people are. During dramatic population movements, and while the national population is growing, we have initiated only a handful of new churches a year. In rough and incomplete form, Dr. Douglas W. Johnson, research analyst for the Board of Global Ministries, charts what we have been doing (See Chart #4, p. 25).

A few observations: Our researchers, like Dr. Johnson, are struggling to gain accurate information because our records are incomplete. Churches without numbers are "lost." That weakness reflects lack of concern. Also, during high mobility and population growth years, 1969–76, we started fewer than two churches a month in the entire nation.

In spite of Ethnic Minority Local Church (EMLC) emphasis, we have begun a mere handful of Hispanic, Native American, and black congregations. Finally, if it were not for the Koreans, who are basically self-starters, we would not have made a significant trend adjustment yet. Deduct those ninety-three Korean churches from the yearly totals and observe that we are not yet awake in new congregational development.

NEW CHURCH DEVELOPMENT

(Chart #4)

YEAR	NUMBER OF CHURCHES STARTED	WITHOUT CHURCH NUMBERS	ETHNIC			
			ASIAN	HISPANIC	BLACK	NATIVE AMERICAN
1966	68	14	1		1	
1967	62	12		2		
1968	37	10				
1969	24	5				
1970	20	8		1		
1971	10	4				
1972	20	2				
1973	18	1				
1974	19	3				
1975	22	2				
1976	24	4	5	3		
1977	42	5	15			2
1978	44	6	6	2		
1979	33	4	11			
1980	43	8	18	1		
1981	46	5	11			
1982	55	14	17	6		1
1983*	39	9	9	3		
TOTALS	626	116	93	18	1	3

*Figures for 1984-85 are unavailable in this form.

COMPILED BY DR. DOUGLAS JOHNSON
GENERAL BOARD OF GLOBAL MINISTRIES

Twenty Million Members

At the General Conference, late at night, tired and muddle-brained, one thousand delegates were asked to set a goal of twenty million members by 1992. The inspiration came from the Koreans. To oppose it would be like boycotting baseball or banning apple pie. We raised our hands. The motion passed. A committee was formed. I was elected chair.

Since that humid night in Baltimore in May 1984, we have lost fifty thousand members and are continuing to hemorrhage at the rate of a thousand members a week. The "average" United Methodist Church has 245 members. We are, in effect, closing the equivalent of three "average" churches each week in the United States.

"But we are concerned," you say. "We did vote to change our posture from decline to growth. Many people are being aroused by the Spirit of God." True, but feeble, with all the power of a person whistling on a dark night while walking through a cemetery.

Dr. Warren Hartman, our most knowledgeable statistician with the General Board of Discipleship, informed me that many people are appalled by the magnitude of the goal that was adopted and by the seeming assumption that a twenty-three year long downward trend could be reversed by legislative action. Dr. Lyle Schaller, in an extremely pessimistic personal letter, wrote: "I am convinced that the membership decline of the denomination is systemic, not a brief passing phenomenon." When asked what he would do if he were asked to raise up twenty million members for The United Methodist Church by 1992, Bishop Mortmer Arias answered, "Decline! Resign! Laugh! Pray! Start working like mad right away!"

But my concern is not that we fail to have twenty million members by 1992; for us that is a ludicrous goal, more of a handicap than a help. Our great danger is that we cannot even turn ourselves around. We do not produce because we are misfocused. We are like modern couples who decide not to have children because they want to find themselves.

I suppose we could gain some encouragement by studying other declining denominations. The Episcopalians, the Presbyterians, and the Disciples are all in decline, and, in fact, more severely than we are, if that is any comfort. But that exercise is fruitless. Those of us known as "mainline" denominations are now called "old line." In 1920, mainline bodies constituted 76 percent of the U. S. Protestant population, but by 1984, that figure had fallen to 53 percent (reported by Harvard University's William Hutchinson). Many younger, more vigorous, more zealous growth-oriented groups are converting significant numbers of disciples. The Assembly of God church has nearly doubled in the last fifteen years. The Southern Baptists, the Church of the Nazarene, the Salvation Army, and the Church of Jesus Christ of the Latter Day Saints show consistently strong growth patterns.

At the pool of Bethesda, the water bubbled and released its healing powers. The water is swirling today. The Holy Spirit is active all over the world. People are being healed. Spiritually hungry, hurting men and women are being converted. Churches are being revitalized. Faith flourishes. Dead congregations are being brought to life, some even among the United Methodists.

We are in a Great Awakening in America. More interest is being expressed in religion than there has been in a hundred years. The secular media, seemingly surprised, asks questions about religion. Television and newspapers report what the churches are doing, because people want to know. The hunger for spiritual sustenance is everywhere. People pore over the Scriptures. The spiritual vacuum in the land is demanding to be filled. Sinsick souls, suffering souls, struggling souls are crying out for help. But our denomination is not responding as it ought.

Our United Methodist timetable, I think, is the word of Jesus in the parable of the vineyard.

27

> There was once a man who had a fig tree growing in his vineyard. He went looking for figs on it but found none. So he said to his gardener, "Look, for three years I have been coming here looking for figs on this fig tree, and I haven't found any. Cut it down! Why should it go on using up the soil?" But the gardener answered, "Leave it alone, sir, just one more year; I will dig around it and put in some fertilizer. Then if the tree bears figs next year, so much the better; if not, then you can have it cut down." (LUKE 13:6-9)

God may not have need of the vine called United Methodism in America. He can raise up other groups. Christ will sustain his church and all the gates of hell will not prevail against it. But he can lop off branches that bear no fruit; he can cut down our vine if it fails to produce.

How much more time do we have? We are impotent lying beside the pool; make no mistake about it. But the Spirit is moving in the waters. It is no longer adequate for us to make excuses or to bemoan that others go into the water before us. Our cry now is for the Savior to give us the power. We need Jesus to say to us, as he did to the palsy-sick man in Capernaum, "Your sins are forgiven. . . . Get up, pick up your mat and walk" (Mark 2:9).

A
CHURCH
OUT OF FOCUS

L ike someone looking through a pair of binoculars that are out of focus, so are we not seeing clearly. We "look but we do not see," we "listen but we do not hear." Our attention is directed elsewhere. The essentials go undone. We hammer on the iron, but like a blacksmith with sweat in his eyes, we hammer where the iron is cold. There is hope for our church, but it will require a new vision. Right now we are not seeing clearly.

A Church Turned Inward

Perhaps it is our nearsightedness that has made us a church turned inward. Our energies and resources are expended internally. The machinery of the church receives unbelievable attention; we scurry about oiling the wheels of the organizational structure. Originally, we were called *Methodists* because we had a plan, an organization, a *method*. But now our methodology approaches madness, our organizational genius consumes our most sophisticated talent. Our structure has become an end in itself, not a means of saving the world.

I became intensely aware of this myopia when I was a pastor. The evangelism committee met, but did not make any calls. The social concerns commission gathered, but did not write any letters. The educational leaders complained about scriptural illiteracy, but did not read from the Bible. The Council on Ministries assembled to hear reports from the committees but took little action. The Administrative Board sat in session to approve the budget, but no one was saved. We went home tired, thinking we had done our church work.

Annual conferences are plagued by housekeeping chores. Years ago, conferences would sponsor great missionary rallies, intensive youth programs, or significant evangelistic thrusts. Now, in most conferences, committees set philosophical objectives, prepare budgets, interact with other committees, and achieve very little. Most of the money is spent on mileage and meals. In times past, conference committees guided hospitals, camps, and colleges. Now, high-powered administrators and strong boards of trustees do that work, yet the committees still meet. Earlier, conference boards of education nourished thousands of volunteer teachers with workshops, teacher training events, and lab schools. Now, with a de-emphasis on Christian education and with subcommittees reporting to other committees who report to the Conference Council on Ministries, not much happens—squirrels chase other squirrels around the trees. I was intrigued by Bishop Underwood of Louisiana simply asking his cabinet to set a goal of one hundred fifty new adult classes. The cabinet argued it couldn't be done. The bishop urged them to try. He wrote about and affirmed the successes of various churches, and the result was almost a *doubling* of the one hundred fifty-class goal. There was more action than if a hundred committees had met.

The General Church is caught up in its own machinery. It is so complicated and so irrelevant to the local church that most pastors ignore it. Ours is a fast-moving television age; yet, we are still cranking out tired journals that few people read. Most of them are subsidized because they don't sell. Periodicals pile up on the pastor's desk, often unread.

The organizational wheels keep turning, budgets are prepared, personnel are employed, administrative turf is protected. To those in the local church, it doesn't matter much; it's like the committees of Congress—interesting, but a long way off. However, the local church, like the taxpayer, pays the bills.

If we were in a business model, instead of a governmental one, we would streamline the process out of sheer economic necessity. Our boards would make policy; our administrators would manage the organization; our chief executives would hold the ship on course.

John and Charles Wesley encountered the same problem. They rejected organizational complexity. In Bristol, on the first of August in 1745, in the "New Room," the two brothers met with nine other preachers. The names of fourteen assistants were read, and a new rule was added to the twelve they had adopted the year before. It read: "You have nothing to do but to save souls; therefore, spend and be spent in this work. And go always, not only to those who need you, but to those who need you most."

Busyness

Most pastors are not lazy; they are busy. But they are not busy making new disciples or busy helping the lay people learn how to make disciples. Ministers are hurrying about caring for the surviving fellowship. Some experts believe that the typical pastor spends 97 percent of his or her parish time in nurture of members; that is, they are laboring in pastoral care, administration, teaching, and preaching to those who are already members of the church. This "sheepdog" strategy of keeping the flock rounded up is based on a nineteenth-century concept of ministry. It works well in a rural setting where the minister preaches on Sunday and calls on the sick and shut-in during the week. However, as the congregation grows larger, or as the setting becomes more urban, he or she must run faster, see more people, and touch more administrative bases. The pastor is spread too thin. People fall through the cracks.

31

This model was intensified by the pastoral care emphasis that emerged following World War II. My clergy generation is the product of the Clinical Pastoral Education (CPE) mode of training. It did us some good; it took us out of the authoritarian, "know all the answers" posture, and it encouraged us to be empathetic, compassionate, and nondirective. It not only taught us to care for trembling, troubled souls, but it also prepared us to care for people on a one-to-one basis. It did not teach us how to build a supportive community. It did teach us how to listen, but not how to make disciples or how to train others to make disciples. In short, it created busy pastors, hurrying from one troubled person to another, willing to listen and trying to provide emotional undergirding all by ourselves.

When John Wesley was asked by converts for personal spiritual guidance, he at first met with each one privately. Quickly he realized that was hopeless, so he asked inquirers to meet with him as a group on Thursday nights. Great good was accomplished. When the group became too large, he asked others to help in the nurturing process. Eventually the class meetings were formed, and class leaders guided the group experience, kept an eye on the members, and reported directly to the ministers of the societies. It is easy to see, as David Michael Henderson observes, that these classes in early British Methodism soon became the primary means for maintaining pastoral contact and providing group accountability and support for members of the Methodist societies.

Pastors are busy trying to care for their members, the members are content to be looked after, and the world goes to hell on a bobsled. I'm reminded of the advice Ernest Hemingway is reported to have given to Marlene Dietrich. He said, "My dear, never confuse motion with action."

Recently the Jehovah's Witnesses came to our city to build a new church building. A local newspaper article read: *How many Jehovah's Witnesses does it take to build a church?* The Answer: *Eight hundred—but they do it in forty-eight hours!* Most of the account focused on the teamwork, the spirit of goodwill, and the amazing achievement of building a church from Friday to Sunday. Granted that most of the building material had been cut and prepared ahead of time, still the whole thing was newsworthy. What intrigued me most was a comment by one of the laymen when he said, "We want to construct the building as quickly as possible, so that we can get back to our primary task, which is witnessing for the Lord." That layman sharply defined his priorities. Even building a church would not divert his spiritual energies for long. Being busy in church work is not good enough.

Democracy in the Church

Where did we get the idea that we should run a church the way Congress runs the government? A layman, and a great friend of mine, gave me a sign which he placed on my desk. It reads, "For God so loved the world that He didn't send a committee." We are afraid to let individuals decide; we want to have committee meetings.

Sometimes people in leadership roles simply have to make decisions. For example, when the Methodist Church because united in 1939, bishops lost the power to determine the number of districts in an Annual Conference. With the decline of our denomination, and with severe shifts in population, redistricting could lessen apportionments and give better supervision. Some of our best personnel could be placed back in to the local church where they are desperately needed. Some bishops could save their conferences 100,000 to 200,000 dollars a year by redefining their districts. The task is a proper one for an administrator, but now action by the Annual Conferences is required. Historic sentiment and regional pride create endless debate. Many pastors hope to become District Superintendents; if a slot is removed, a possible promotion is eliminated. We can no longer afford these political, emotional, and promotional luxuries. United Methodists need to become "lean" again. That won't be achieved by majority vote.

33

The Saving Power of God

Elton Trueblood used to say that we are a "cut flower" culture, drawing on the spiritual resources of earlier roots. The image is appropriate for our church, for we are a cut flower church, showing certain manifestations of the Gospel, but separated from our nourishment. Trueblood observes that we "cannot reasonably expect to erect a constantly expanding structure of social activism upon a constantly diminishing foundation of faith."

John Wesley feared that something like this might happen. He wrote in 1786, "I am not afraid that the people called Methodists should ever cease to exist either in Europe or America. But I am afraid, lest they should only exist as a dead sect, having the form of religion without the power."

If I were to attend fifty United Methodist churches next Sunday morning, quiet as a church mouse, but with ears cocked like a newspaper reporter, what would I hear? Mostly the sermons would expound ethical implications of the Gospel. The imperative mood would be strong. The text would be Romans 12:1, "Offer yourselves as a living sacrifice to God." Or Ephesians 4:1, "I urge you . . . live a life that measures up to the standard God set when he called you."

The sermons would be good for me, for they would urge me to be kinder to my immediate associates, and I need that. They would insist that I care more about God's children who are dying of famine, and, after a plethora of covered-dish dinners, I need that. They would remind me that we live under a nuclear cloud, and I must not neglect "those things that make for peace." The less effective sermons would encourage me to love my neighbor, but would not be specific and would contain little passion. The more effective ones would clearly reveal my callous self-preoccupation, my pride, my condescending sexism, and my racism. The preacher would lift up my responsibilities. In short, I would be told what I should do; the sermon would deal with my response to Jesus Christ.

However, the sermon, in all likelihood, would not tell me what God is doing to me, in me, through me, for me. The preacher would not tell me how God changes the sinful heart into a heart of faith and love. Is God at work in the world? Is God at work in the church? Is God at work in me? Tell me what God is doing right here and now!

In looking at my own preaching, I find an over-emphasis on ethics and an under-emphasis on Gospel. It is as if we preachers assumed that all people are Christian, and our job is to spur them on. Paul has, midway in many of his letters, a mighty *therefore*. The first half of the letters proclaim what God has done, is doing, and will do for us and for the world in Christ Jesus. The last half spell out areas of our response. The letter to the Ephesians also is built precisely in this way—three chapters about what God is doing, and three chapters about what Christians ought to be doing. The word *therefore* (Ephesians 4:1) is the hinge on which the scriptural door turns. In our churches, we are not proclaiming what God is doing; we are emphasizing human response. We are like cut flowers, no longer nourished by the amazing grace that caused us to blossom in the first place. We act theologically, as if everyone were a child of the kingdom. Yet, Christ has forcefully proclaimed that except we become converted and become as little children, we shall not enter the kingdom of God.

In *Moral Man and Immoral Society,* Reinhold Niebuhr called us to social repentance. We should have repented and shouted like Isaiah: "I am doomed because every word that passes my lips is sinful, and I live among a people whose every word is sinful" (Isaiah 6:5). Then, feeling the burning coal of atonement on our lips, we should have rushed out to tell others about the fiery altar of grace.

When Augustine read the prologue of John's Gospel, he saw that he had to choose between heaven and hell, between brothels and the bridegroom, between the philosophies of stoicism and the intrusion of the Savior. Nowhere else in all the writings of the world, he said, is it written, "the Word became flesh." The kingdom broke in upon him, and this world's hold upon him was broken.

The theological crisis is precisely whether we are Wesleyans or not. Historians say that in John and Charles Wesley's experiences, and in the sermons and music that flowed forth, the birthday of a Christian shifted from the time of his baptism to that of conversion, and in that change the dividing line of two great systems was crossed. We will have to decide whether a Christian is someone born in America and baptized by water or a person who knows the gracious work of Christ in his or her heart.

Our Social Witness

The people called Methodists are neither pietists nor mystics. Wesley made sure of that. He would not let us be concerned only with our individual spiritual experiences. He not only offered Christ to the people, but he also collected coal for their stoves and organized schools for their children. We are made forever aware of injustice by his powerful letter to William Wilburforce, his last handwritten letter, denouncing the American slave traffic as the "vilest thing that ever saw the sun."

E. Stanley Jones said once that we believe in the "warm heart and the world parish," in the "inward experience and the outward expression." We never were and we never can be a *spiritual* religion unattached to our flesh-and-blood world. We are to "work out our salvation in fear and trembling" as social, economic, and political persons.

Historians remind us that Susanna and Samuel, John's mother and father, once quarreled over politics and did not sleep together for a considerable time. Their reconciliation of love (not of politics) caused John to be conceived. It will always be difficult for Wesley's followers to keep politics out of religion. But something has gone askew.

Our Limited Political Power

The public pronouncements of our boards and agencies—even those of the Council of Bishops—now have little power. Why is that?

First of all, we are now a smaller denomination with less influence. Consider this analogy: Recently, in the midst of our farm crisis, President Reagan was quoted as saying, "Let's keep the grain and export the farmers." I was aghast. I grew up in an agricultural state and worked my way through college by baling alfalfa hay. I couldn't believe the president could get away with what he said. I waited for a tumultuous uproar in response to such a callous comment. There was none. Again I was surprised—until I began to think. In 1900 over 90 percent of Americans lived on the farm. Today, they make up only about 3 percent. Politically that is an insignificant number. That is about how many United Methodists we have—about 3 to 4 percent—a rather insignificant number. We can make few demands.

Second, we are politically weak because the leadership of the church often does not speak for the membership. The politicians know that a bishop has only one vote. Politicians read the letters that come from mechanics and housewives in their districts. Some of the letters are from United Methodists. What those letters say and what the public pronouncements say are often at variance. The politicians listen to the people.

Why is there a disparate viewpoint? I think there are several reasons. One is that our leadership is now far removed from the people. General agency staff, bishops, even elected lay and clergy delegates to various conferences are once or twice removed from the grassroots—New York is a long way from Dumas, Arkansas. The 727 jet that whisks the bishop to the wood paneled offices in Nashville or the marbled halls of Washington, D.C., is a long way from the pick-up trucks parked for coffee at Sadie's Cafe.

A kind of presumptuousness has developed that "papa

37

knows best." Pronouncements proliferate, and the people ask, "Why didn't I have a voice in that? Nobody asked me." It is time for pronouncements to be replaced by pastoral letters so that communication can be restored to the local churches. Besides, the people in the local community often have better facts and more relevant data. That information needs to flow "upward" as well as pronouncements coming "down." Real power today is in the neighborhoods of America. Despite the sophistication of our major cities, almost nothing starts there. America is a *bottom up* society. If we are to make social and political impact today, it must come from the local congregations.

Conversion of Social Conscience

We act as if citizens of our country were converted Christians, seeing political events through the eyes of Christ. They are not. Until we convert non-Christians, how can we expect them to agree with our social vision? They still see through unredeemed eyes. Self-interest plagues us all, but controls those untouched by Christ. "Whoever does not have the Spirit cannot receive the gifts that come from God's Spirit . . . they are nonsense to him, because their value can be judged only on a spiritual basis" (I Corinthians 2:14).

The early societies and classes performed powerfully in remaking the social conscience. The Wesleyan classes sought to teach new Methodists the conduct and behavior of Christians. If we want Americans to agree with our social and political perspectives, we must first help them to "see" with the eyes of Christ. That means making disciples and teaching them what Christ has taught us.

At present we are perceived by the world as a denomination with a "knee jerk" political persuasion. That is an erroneous opinion because our people have many public viewpoints. But it is our public image. One keen observer said that The United Methodist Church is perceived by secular society not as a people of God, but as a political movement. Dr. Albert Outler, in a brilliant address on a free church in a free state, said that churches that act as if they are just another political party lose both their character and their clout. When a church thinks of itself as a political advocate, as our United Methodist Church has done, its rewards inevitably are political.

Preoccupation

Our social witness becomes lopsided in two forms. The first is "far off"; the second is "near." By "far off" I mean that church leaders have become preoccupied with issues that are distant from the average person. Yale University professor Halford Luccock used to call that *Afghanistanism*, meaning some place so far away that people didn't know where it was and didn't care very much. Now that Afghanistan is daily in our papers because of the Russian invasion there, the word is rendered useless, but the idea remains. Leadership gets so excited that our pulse elevates over a boycott of grapes or a military coup in Liberia. But the people in our churches wonder why the sixteen-year-old down the block is on drugs, whether they could have helped the farm implement dealer before he committed suicide, or if the neighborhood school can survive. The spotlight of the church's concern seems to shine on some distant shore. A pastor recently asked me, "What are the hot issues right now?" I said, "Tell me what you mean." He responded, "Well, I've preached on South Africa, Central America, and Ethiopia, and you've been going to national meetings. I thought you could help me know where the action is. I've run out of sermons."

Issues far off are often exotic, like planting orchids. Problems at home are ordinary, like growing geraniums. But the at-homeness is where our people are, and they are going to heaven or hell in the midst of those issues. Some of our people are not getting much help in their life battles.

Jesus put the perspective properly, for he began at home and gradually moved outward, "When the Holy Spirit comes upon you, you will be filled with power, and you will be witnesses for me in Jerusalem and in all of Judea and Samaria, and to the ends of the earth" (Acts 1:8). Like a rock thrown into a lake, the splash is greatest where the rock lands, but the concentric circles make their gentle waves all the way to the shore. So ought our social witness to be.

By "near," I mean within the human heart. When Wesley insisted, "We have nothing to do but to save souls," he was not denying the social witness. He was simply putting matters in right perspective.

We have become preoccupied with politics. We are energized by economic leverages. We are consumed in cultural realignments. But we have forgotten how to mediate the change which God works in the heart through faith in Christ. We have forgotten how to do it with the poor, the dispossessed, the ethnic minorities, the people with handicapping conditions right in our own home towns. We pass resolutions about the poor, but we do not invite them into our churches. We give bread, but we do not break bread with them. We will be judged as to whether we gave bread to the hungry. Our Lord did and so will we. But "man cannot live on bread alone, but needs every word that God speaks" (Matthew 4:4). Jesus himself resisted the temptation to limit his ministry to giving bread alone. So must we.

Nor do we hide our gospel in order to make converts. We publish our good tidings in the full light of the sun. Baptist preacher Jimmy Allen is right in arguing for social involvement while evangelizing. Chided for a strong statement on racial justice that, said his critic, would lessen the number of Baptist converts, Allen replied, "Evangelism is not tricking people into signing a policy and then letting them discover the small print."

As Wesleyans, we believe we have tasted the kingdom where racial injustices disappear, where forgiveness fosters peace, where food is shared with neighbors, where women and men are children of God. We don't hide the kingdom when we draw disciples to the king.

Reinhold Niebuhr, who can never be accused of being a pietist, wrote in 1926:

40

That resolution which we passed in our pastor's meeting calling upon the police to be more rigorous in the enforcement of law, is a nice admission of defeat upon the part of the church. Every one of our cities has a crime problem, not so much because the police are not vigilant as because great masses of men in an urban community are undisciplined and chaotic souls. . . . There is something very pathetic about the efforts of almost everyone of our large cities to restore by police coercion what has been lost by the decay of moral and cultural traditions. . . . The church cannot recoup its failures by giving advice to the police department. The priest as a sublimated policeman is a sorry spectacle. *Leaves from the Notebooks of a Tamed Cynic*

As I reread this passage from my worn copy of the book, I remembered a boy who stood before the juvenile judge a few years ago. The boy had broken into a cigarette machine and stolen a few dollars. His father and I stood with him. The boy was a member of a church school and the local Boy Scout troop. The judge asked him if he knew the Ten Commandments. The kid said no. He later admitted to me that he knew some of them, but was afraid he would be called upon to recite them. The judge asked me, his pastor, why the boy didn't know them, and I was more speechless than the boy. Then the judge explained that this was the first boy he could remember standing before his bench who had been active in Sunday school.

Not many kids are in the church or Sunday schools of our land today—maybe 15 percent on any given Sunday morning. Why is that? With a United Methodist Church in every hamlet, town, and city in America, don't we care if the kids live or die?

Basically we live in an unconverted generation, although the religious trappings are there. People still sing "Silent Night" at Christmas time, and women wear crosses around their necks. But across our country, 40 percent of the people profess no church affiliation at all. On any given Sunday, less than 3.5 million United Methodists are in worship. By my calculation about 175 million Americans are not in a worship service on

Saturday or Sunday in the synagogues and churches of America.

Could it be that we are preoccupied with the political process? I am amused at the Moral Majority and some other conservatives who enter the political fray with intensity. They used to stand aloof and criticize the United Methodists for getting involved in politics. Now they are in hook, line, and sinker. At the moment, they have taken the political initiatives away from us because they have the power to do so. They are also in harmony with the conservative mood of our country. But they will be burned, just as we have been burned, if they forget their main purpose—to help people find God. I fear they have already fallen, lured by the bitch goddess, success.

Our Social Service

When did it happen—the gradual shift from conversion to compassion? Or to say it differently, when did we become primarily concerned with giving bread and begin to neglect the giving of the bread of life?

People faddishly use the phrase, "to be in ministry." What does it mean? The core meaning emerges in both content and emotion from Matthew, "I was hungry and you fed me, thirsty and you gave me a drink; I was a stranger and you received me in your homes, naked and you clothed me; I was sick and you took care of me, in prison and you visited me" (Matthew 25:35-36).

To be in ministry, for countless pastors and their congregations, means to provide a day-care center, a child or women's abuse refuge, a food pantry, a clothing outlet, a recreational program for the elderly, or a social service program. The motivation is Wesleyan and biblical, but we have made social service fundamental to, rather than flowing from, our ministry. Compassionate ministries now are the *focus* rather than the *fruit* of our faith.

The distinction is all important. Christ calls us to "make disciples," and in the process of making disciples, we feed, clothe, visit, and welcome. Moreover, the new disciples, as they are learning how to make other disciples, show the fruit of their newfound faith and fellowship by spinning off caring concerns, for "faith without actions is dead" (James 2:26b).

We fell into a trap. First we thought that one way to convert was to be mutely kind. We often quoted Edgar A. Guest "I'd rather see a sermon than hear one any day." We mean by *seeing* a sermon to do deeds of compassion. We actually thought we could transform human hearts by philanthropy. This emphasis was a reaction to hard-nosed evangelism that "preached the blood of Christ" but left the hungry without food and the naked without clothes. How often missionaries would tell us, "You can't preach the love of Christ to native people who are wracked with disease, bloated with malnutrition, or ignorant of basic learning. First you must share love, and then you can share Christ." That was true, but that concept still meant that our goal was to help people experience God in Christ. Compassion opened the door for change. It also exhibited the normal Christian life-style of caring behavior. But the goal to "publish glad tidings of redemption and release" was the central and ultimate goal.

Gradually we were lulled into thinking that concern for the poor and needy would draw them automatically to consecration and commitment. Discipleship would happen by osmosis if we showed our love. But giving bread is not the same as breaking bread, and providing social service is not the same as offering salvation.

For ten years a downtown congregation conducted a day-care center. Other churches gave support. A semi-autonomous board of directors governed the enterprise. Every morning, beginning at 6:30 A.M., the three, four and five-year-olds were dropped off by their working parents. About thirty-five children a day received love, good food, and appropriate preschool experiences in a safe, clean, and educational environment. Divorced mothers and fathers said it was a lifesaver. Scholarships subsidized the costs for many children whose single parents were barely keeping their financial heads above water. "Why should

43

the big educational wing of the church stand empty all week long when we could be serving people?" was an oft-repeated supportive argument. Building supplies and utilities were provided without cost. The center became the model for first class day-care for the city.

But none of the families joined the church, not a single new member. Some of the teachers were members. Occasionally a child already in the congregation took part in the day-care program. But the day-care was not a form of evangelization.

Now, before you explode and say, "But it was a terrific ministry well worth the cost," let me explain. You are right! It was valuable in and of itself. But many thought it was a port of entry into the fellowship. It was not.

Why? For two reasons, I think. First, social service generally is not evangelism. When we do provide social services, as we must if we are to obey our Lord, we ought not to confuse our thinking. Some of the dynamics in compassion actually militate against personal acceptance. Often the "givers" convey an air of condescension. Usually the "receivers" express an attitude of defensiveness. The social, economic, and educational gulfs are difficult to bridge.

In our urban ministries, I have watched scores of people standing in line to receive a sackful of groceries provided by caring people. But the recipients are grim faced, with eyes down, hoping to get the food and go home with a minimum of hassle. It is degrading to have to take a handout, but if a mother's babies are crying, and she is out of milk, she accepts the gift. But she does not fall in love with God or with the giver. In addition, our ecumenical cooperation can cause us to be hesitant about proselytizing, even though many children and their parents have neither religious commitment nor congregational affiliation.

The second reason is that we do not fulfill the whole commandment. We omit "I was a stranger and you welcomed me." We do not go far enough. Looking back, we see that the members and the pastor of the church did not try very hard to bring people from the day-care program or from the grocery ministry into the congregation. They were not called in their homes, inviting the children to Sunday school. They were not personally helped to feel welcome to church gatherings. In short, the members and the pastor were not aggressive in offering the broken bread of fellowship to the parents.

Why not? Because the vision was so limited the members thought they were being "Christian." They were "in ministry." In fact, they were, in the name of service, blind to the command of Jesus to make disciples. They were callous in their pride, subtly opening the church doors but not opening their hearts to hurting people. They thought they were in mission when they were just giving alms.

One day it was reported that a three-year-old child came to the center bruised and badly beaten. "What should we do?" the director asked. She was urged to report the matter to the authorities immediately. She did. A few weeks later, a state social worker called in the home and learned that the child's mother was living with a man who sometimes was angry and violent with the children. A formal report was filed. Several weeks passed. One morning, the news came that the child was dead. She had been beaten to death by her mother's friend, right in her own home. The entire event went practically unnoticed in the congregation's experience, like so many events of violence in the city. Was there a chance that Christ Jesus could have saved child, mother, and man, if they had been offered more than an open building from 6:00 A.M. to 6:00 P.M.? What if the household had been aggressively pursued for fellowship? What if the central concern had been the change which God works in the human heart through faith in Christ?

When the camera is out of focus, many people want to throw the camera away. Some people, frustrated at membership decline, want to abandon social witness or social service and "do evangelism." Other people, intent on the inertia of the status quo, like a horse with blinders on will try to plow ahead until we disappear. The answer will be to refocus, to put priorities on our performance.

In John's Gospel Jesus whispers: "'Peace be with you. As the Father sent me, so I send you.' Then he breathed on them and said, 'Receive the Holy Spirit. If you forgive people's sins, they are forgiven'" (John 20:21-23a).

In Matthew's Gospel, Jesus stands on the hilltop like a general before the battle and commissions us: "Go, then, to all peoples everywhere and make them my disciples: baptize them in the name of the Father, the Son and the Holy Spirit, and teach them to obey everything I have commanded you. And I will be with you always, to the end of the age" (Matthew 28:19-20).

If we are to be faithful to the great commission, we will continue to feed the hungry, heal the sick, and clothe the naked. We will be calling new converts into our total work of conversion and compassion while we are making disciples.

WHO'S MINDING
THE STORE?

mmediately after I was consecrated a bishop, a friend
came by to see me. He was president and CEO of a major
corporation, a marvelous Christian, and a great
churchman. He went right to the point; he said, "Dick,
any large company that has a track record like The
United Methodist Church, whose charts show steady
decline, would have been called on the carpet long ago.
The board of directors would have demanded emergency
meetings, and the corporate executives would have
been held accountable. Consultants would have been
brought in. Heads would roll. It would not be business
as usual."

Those of us in places of leadership in The United
Methodist Church must assume a great deal of responsibility for the decline of our denomination. Bishops, members
of general boards, key laypersons, district superintendents, and pastors have focused on many matters, but not
on the health and well-being of the local church.

During the annual conference, when the statistician
finished reading the negative report to the conference, one
bishop got up from his chair and stepped to the floor of the
conference. He then led the entire body in a service of
contrition. With dignity and power, he guided a confession

of sins for failing to lead men and women, girls and boys into a saving relationship with God and into a fellowship experience in the church of Jesus Christ.

An Informed Leadership

I used to think that John Wesley and Francis Asbury rode their horses a quarter of a million miles or so because they loved to preach. Now I realize that, as leaders of the movement, they needed to know what was going on. They rode to observe the vital signs of the movement as well as to censure and encourage the people; it was literally a seat of the pants form of leadership. Today, in a world of instant communications, we are abysmally ignorant of the vitality of our churches. The leaders cannot lead until first they know what is happening.

When Lee Iacocca became president of Chrysler Corporation, he immediately demanded essential information. It was not available. He realized that one reason Chrysler was bankrupt was because no one knew what was going on. No wonder he fired thirty-two vice presidents in thirty-five months. Look at our own ignorance:

—How many youth attend church camp each year? Nobody knows.

—How many preschool children do we have in our church schools? Nobody knows.

—How many preschools do we have? Nobody knows.

—How many children attend Vacation Bible School? It is one of our most vital ways of reaching unchurched families. No figures are available.

—How many women attend the United Methodist Women's meetings? Nobody knows.

—How many men participated in United Methodist Men? Nobody knows.

—How many youth take part in our Sunday evening youth fellowship? Nobody knows.

—Some observers believe that the active youth in our youth fellowship are not active adults in our churches ten years later. Is that true? Nobody knows.

—How old is our membership? Nobody knows.

It is no wonder that some people are asking, "Who's minding the store?"

Other data are sketchy. How many churches have we closed in twenty years? Estimates vary from three to five thousand. How many churches have we started? About seven hundred forty, according to the general minutes.

What about our ethnic minority churches? The Korean congregations are growing in the United States, but we cannot locate, coordinate, or communicate with many of them. Some are Methodist, some are United Methodist, some are Korean Methodist, some are independent Methodist, some are house churches. Our task is an immediate effort to know, to understand, and to encourage them.

The Numbers

I don't believe in the numbers game. So goes a popular slogan. If that means numbers where there are no people, a mathematical falsehood, neither do I. If it means adding names just to get numbers, without converting or caring, I am equally offended. The last thing we need is a membership drive—send in your name and a box top and you belong, along with millions of others, to the Captain Midnight Club.

However, leadership must know the numbers, and it is no game. The good shepherd knows his sheep—by number and by name. Let me refer again to Halford Luccock, my one-time professor and a notorious burster of ecclesiastical bubbles. He used to joke about our "Methodist Statistical Church." He claimed that we tabulated everything that could be measured. But if it were true then, it's not true now. Today we are walking in the dark, ignorant of many of our most vital enterprises.

Of course, there are always those who resist statistics, some because they don't want to be held accountable. Others want only to relate personally to Tom Smith and Mary Jones and not to abstractions. But leadership has to know what's going on. You can't navigate the ship without continually reading the numbers and charting the course. Ignorance of statistics is ultimately a cheap cop-out for not caring whether an organization lives or dies. In statistics, people, for a moment, are translated into conceptual data, and any enterprise that ignores essential data travels the road to oblivion.

Dr. William Hinson of Houston told me of a trip he once took with sixty-four teenagers to Europe. His consuming goal was to get them there and back, safe and sound, all in one piece. As he stood at the airport gate in London, ready to return, he listened as the final boarding was called for their flight. Almost ready to breathe a sigh of relief, he decided to count the kids one more time. He counted—sixty-three. Again—sixty-three. One was missing! The first passengers were boarding, but he turned and began running back, back through security, yelling in each rest-room, back to the center of the airport, running, calling, glancing frantically. Suddenly he saw her—a sixteen-year-old girl casually buying a candy bar and a movie magazine, seemingly oblivious to time or place. He grabbed her hand, and together they ran toward the gate. The attendant was closing the door as they squeezed in. All was well. The girl had been saved by the count. Dr. Hinson would not have gone home until she was found.

Counting is important in the Bible. The number *1* is important. It is a holy number, often referring to God. It is a precious number, reflecting the eternal significance of a single soul. A man had two sons. When one rebelled and left home, the father knew it. He waited anxiously until the one came back. A woman had ten coins. One was missing; she knew by counting. She feverishly swept the house until she found it. A shepherd had one hundred sheep. One had strayed; the shepherd knew because he counted. He may have counted twice to be sure. Then he left the ninety-nine to search for the one that was lost. He would not go on until the missing sheep was found.

Numbers help us evaluate the situation. When Judas betrayed Jesus and was lost, Peter insisted, "May someone else take his place of service" (Acts 1:20). Straws were drawn by two witnesses to the resurrection, and Matthias was chosen. Eleven was not enough. The full strength of twelve was necessary to change the world.

As the early church grew, it kept statistics. In the Upper Room, Peter stood before the assembled brotherhood, about one hundred twenty in all (Acts 1:15). Following Peter's Pentecost sermon in Jerusalem, those who accepted his word were baptized and some three thousand were added to the number that day. Later, after Christ used Peter and John to heal the crippled man by the beautiful gate, Peter preached again, and the number of men reached about five thousand.

In the business world, accounting is absolutely essential for successful enterprise. Many contractors, capable as builders, have gone broke because they didn't keep track of numbers. The best thing a fledgling entrepreneur can do as his or her business expands is to engage an accountant. The figures tell us where we are and what is happening. Financier, and outspoken critic of wasteful government spending, J. Peter Grace states in *Burning Money* that the numbers tell exactly what the situation is. The only way we are going to find out about something is to look at the facts, and the facts are the numbers.

Accountability

But the issue is deeper still. Somebody must be held accountable for the spiritual nurture of every soul. Bishops are supposed to hold the churches accountable. Each episcopal area of the church has a chief pastor, a bishop. The bishop must hold every parish and every pastor accountable for stewardship. No one else can do it.

Many questions need to be asked. Many people need to stand on the carpet as they are questioned.

Look at the record:

Last year's report showed 16,093 churches (42 percent) that did not have a constituency roll (a prospect list)—not even one scribbled on the back of an envelope! No prospect list at all? Do we not care whether our neighbors are brought to Christ? No names in nearly half our churches? To whom do they report their spiritual stewardship?

Bishop Monk Bryan reminded us that his father kept a prayer list of the unsaved who were on his heart. He prayed for each one every day until he had won that person to Christ. Who is doing that today?

Our fires of Wesleyan revival are burning low. Last year's report showed 22,912 churches (60 percent) that did not have a membership training or confirmation class. There was not even one thirteen-year-old boy or girl guided and nurtured into the fellowship of the church. That does not speak of the sloppy, inadequate, short-term classes being taught. Is not this failure of ministry inexcusable?

Incidentally, when we recently urged each church in our area to have a training class, a young woman, part-time local pastor of twenty souls, said to her people that it would be impossible. But a laywoman responded with, "Oh, no, I know of a man right now who wants to be baptized and join the church. You can have a membership training class just for him." That kind of insight and zeal would revitalize the church.

We think of the Southeastern and South Central Jurisdictions as being somewhat evangelical. But both are among the weakest in the nation in number of confirmation classes; nearly 70 percent of the churches in the Southeast are without membership training classes. Both jurisdictions are also among the lowest in the number of persons received by profession of faith in relation to total membership. Migration of population and transfer of membership letters in the Sun Belt states cannot substitute for a careful nurture of persons, preparing them to unite with the church because they believe.

Who is holding our churches accountable? The last report showed that 14,423 churches (38 percent) did not receive one person into the fellowship by profession of faith. Exactly 25,662 churches (over 67 percent) received four persons or less. What are they doing?

I have been in big churches and little churches. I have yet to see a church located in an area where there are no sinners to be converted, no suffering souls to be comforted, no struggling people to be strengthened by the fellowship of the church.

America is a tough mission field. Americans are immunized by religious talk, coated with a Christian veneer that keeps us from becoming soundly converted. About eighty-five million people claim no church at all. Surely the church can find one person to invite into its company. Even congregations working and witnessing amid economic depression and population decline may not grow, but they can convert.

If each church in our denomination received one person by profession of faith for every one hundred members, the whole downward trend would be reversed in a single year. Who will see to it that it happens?

Baptism figures are equally sobering. The record shows that 12,026 of our churches (31 percent) did not baptize a single person—infant, child, or adult. Exactly 25,086 churches (66 percent) baptized four persons or fewer—infant, child, or adult—during the past year. Who is holding our feet to the spiritual fire?

Inactive Members

Someone must account for each individual soul. Wesley was a fanatic on the subject. When my wife, Julia, and I visited the "New Room" in Bristol, England, we noted the historic class meeting rolls. Class leaders kept track of twelve to sixteen members with a careful weekly notation, whether they were present and whether they were "paid." The sick were called on. Reporting was made regularly by the class leader to the minister. Accountability was built into the system. No one was lost in the cracks; no one slipped out the back door. If a person left, the leader knew about it. Some did fall away, of course, but not without notice. Today, thousands leave our fellowship unnoticed until it is too late to retrieve them.

Our national membership committee, through the General Board of Discipleship, is exploring a hotline—a telephone plan by which each membership secretary would telephone a central office, either in each state or nationally, to give quick information about a member who is moving to another town or city. In a matter of hours, that information would be relayed to a local church membership secretary and a telephone call would be made while the moving van is still unloading the furniture. Follow-up personal calls would still be made, but we would be giving immediate, concerned pastoral care. What a switch from pastors on one end, trying to keep members on their rolls as long as possible, and pastors on the other end, two years after the fact, "bird-dogging" lost souls who have allowed the trauma of the relocation to isolate them from the church!

Our goal is to get people into heaven, not to sustain burdened membership rolls. Now we have the technology to keep up with people. Of course, Wesley and his class leaders kept up with their people too, by letter, word of mouth and personal associations. But he didn't have nine million or so folks, so we have to be more contemporary. Who will hold our denomination accountable to achieve this important pastoral care task?

The most powerful way to hold the fellowship intact is by face-to-face relationships. I want to explore this method more thoroughly later when we ponder the future of The United Methodist Church in our complex society. But nothing holds a person responsible like a gathering of Christian friends, small enough where each soul is a significant person, known and loved.

What held the people together in the early church? Listen: "They spent their time in learning from the apostles, taking part in the fellowship, and sharing in the fellowship meals and the prayers. . . . All the believers continued together in close fellowship and shared their belongings with one another. . . . Day after day they met as a group in the Temple, and they had their meals together in their homes, eating with glad and humble hearts" (Acts 2:42, 44, 46).

Several members of a certain congregation once reviewed the names of those who had united with the church during the previous six months. They wanted to make sure they were in a face-to-face relationship—adult classes, prayer groups, choirs, circles of the UMW, United Methodist Men, and Bible studies. If they were, they were inevitably active in their worship and in their stewardship of time and money. If not, the people went after them, almost as if they were prospective members, trying once again to make them a part of the "body." Gradually the charge conference removals withered to a tiny number. The back door almost closed.

New Congregations

According to the *Discipline* (p. 268), bishops are supposed to start new churches. The job is tough today, because big money is almost always involved. So are strategy, personnel, and timing. Population shifts occur rapidly. Old city church buildings, in transitional neighborhoods, receive nostalgic loyalty but lack driving evangelical fervor. New urban developments often need twenty years lead time in congregational development planning. Tiny rural churches are sometimes suddenly surrounded by instant urban sprawl and they cannot cope. The conference committees, the cabinet, the district structure, and the general boards require coordination.

But tremendous resources are available—laymen and laywomen who know demographics; churches that want to reach out; the general agencies with evaluation and counseling personnel, architectural guidance, loans, and grants; the Publishing House with a free curriculum—all are willing to help .

The children of darkness are sometimes wiser than the children of light. Modern marketing procedures have much to teach us about church development. We can do it, but someone must challenge our stewardship. Someone must aggressively attack the future.

Negativism

We should expect resistance. Great pressures push hard against disciple-making. Much negative thinking exists. Our momentum for conversion and compassion for people has been hindered by a spirit of negativism that has swept through the church, particularly through the ministry. We have become experts at being critical of all forms of outreach and evangelization. Hindu theologians and teachers sometimes define God by saying what he is not. That is, they say, "God is not this. God is not this. God is not this." It has now become popular for us, particularly for professional ministers, to ridicule every form of disciple making by saying, "Real evangelism isn't this." "You must be born again?—Baptist theology; too dramatic. A bus ministry?—We don't want just kids, we want the whole family. Raise a hand and sing *Praise the Lord?*—Too emotional. Call house-to-house in teams of two like the Mormons?—That's proselytizing. TV evangelism?—They are always asking for money. The four spiritual laws?—simplistic and presumptuous. A two-year confirmation class like the Lutherans?—Too organized; lacks the reality of conversion." The disclaimers go on and on. It is as if we wanted to do away with procreation because sex is involved. In church growth, neither I nor any of us want hucksters. No United Methodist wants to prostitute the gospel. I remember a story told about William Booth, that Methodist preacher who wanted to do evangelism among the "bob-tag and rag-tail" of London. To the woman who criticized his methods of evangelism, he replied, "Madam, I like my way of doing it better than your way of not doing it."

We have much to learn from churches that are growing and helping men and women find God in their lives. We have much to learn from the growing Methodists in the Third World. Methodism is growing in Africa. Methodism is growing in Korea. Methodism is growing in Latin America. Can the parent learn from the children?

Jesus, in the persuasive parable of the talents, proclaimed that if we hide our entrusted resources in the ground, even that which we have will be taken away from us. This is happening now; our Lord said we shall be called into accountability by the master of the house. If we fail in our disciple-making, we shall be cast away and there will be weeping and gnashing of teeth (see Matthew 25:14-30).

Structures

Some of our structures are super. Some of our structures are stupid. Sometimes it is not easy to tell which is which. Independent pastors like Billy Graham and Robert Schuller may stand in amazement at our mighty organizational structures, but maybe they do not know all of our problems.

We have a church in nearly every hamlet, town, and city. Our slogan is *More United Methodist Churches than United States Post Offices.* We have a church in almost every county in the nation.

We have a supervisory system of district superintendents, working as extensions of the chief pastor. They are the heartbeat of Methodism.

We have worked hard and are working harder still to be an inclusive church, making sure that minorities and women are empowered to be part and parcel of leadership. That style is Wesleyan and depicts the wave of the future.

We are a "connection" which is both formal and informal—formal, as in the apportionment system, and informal as a kind of ethos or "networking" in which communication flows day and night.

We have giant general agencies that are the servants of the church, dealing with everything from nuclear war to child abuse, from the preschool curriculum to seminary accreditation.

We have a democratic church governed by laity and clergy. We have a unified church which has brought north and south together, assimilated to some extent the Central Jurisdiction, and joined with the Evangelical United Brethren.

We have a consultative appointment system that, while not perfect, is the best there is. We are mobilized like an army ready for battle. But we are marching backwards. Part of our future requires an overhaul of our structure. Courageous leadership will be required.

Our motivation must be Wesleyan. John Wesley changed his structures, almost against his will, in order to save souls. He didn't want to use women as class leaders, but he did, in "unusual" circumstances. The "unusual" became very normal. He didn't want to use lay preachers, but he did. They were converting sinners. He didn't want to ordain, but he did, for the "fields were white unto the harvest." He didn't want to preach in the open fields, but he did. Thousands listened to the Word, with rivulets of tears cutting the coal dust on their cheeks.

With regard to bending or breaking the structures, Wesley wrote, "I would observe every punctilio or order, except when the salvation of souls is at stake. Then I prefer the end to the means" (Ensley, 1958, p. 39).

We need to make some changes in order to achieve our biblical and Wesleyan goals. The bishops can be chief pastors, responsible for their churches, serving as diligently in their areas as if they were pastors in the local church. Using the district superintendents, the bishop needs to study and supervise each church. Are the outdoor church signs clear and well lighted? Are new church school classes being formed? What is each church's method of disciple-making? When is the confirmation class? Are all rolls, including preparatory membership and constituency, active? Are church school rooms freshly painted and attractively decorated? Is the UMW initiating groups for working women, and are those groups helping women experience faith and fellowship in the church? Is there a ministry to single adults? How strong is the youth program? What specialized training would be helpful? How can the church speak by radio and television in our areas?

The Bishops' Cabinet needs a pool of lay personnel, including diaconal ministers to serve as workers with youth, directors of music, educational assistants, and directors. Tips, suggestions, program ideas, personnel brokerage—such is the stuff of supervision.

Is each church growing? Why not? Do unique circumstances exist? Can outside resources be brought to bear? Will pastors reach out for help and encouragement? The district superintendent increasingly must become a supervisor, striving to work with each pastor to make that pastor successful, just as a life insurance district manager works with his or her salespersons to help them succeed.

That means the bishop will need to spend the bulk of his or her time within the area, and necessarily will need to cut back national and international responsibilities. Just as a pastor must judiciously measure her or his time outside the parish, so, too, the bishops can provide only limited ministry outside their areas. Retired bishops may need to be pressed into duty. Other persons can serve in many of these international posts. Some jobs will wither away. We don't have time to waste. Bishops must help strip down the structures, streamline the districts, and dramatically mobilize the movement.

Somebody must hold us accountable. Recently I was asked by a lay friend, "Who is your boss?" I thought for a moment, then pointed my finger skyward. "God?" he said, surprised. "I guess so," I replied. "No one else ever asks me to report on the seven hundred and ninety-one congregations in Arkansas." Somebody should, perhaps the president of the Council of Bishops, or perhaps the president of each College of Bishops in the jurisdictions, or perhaps a peer relationship, one on one. Remember, as sick as we are, superficial cosmetics won't suffice.

Within the annual conferences, all sorts of structural changes can occur. We should let the administrators manage—cut meals and mileage to a minimum, eliminate as many committees as possible. Our task is to make disciples, not to travel across the state to decide whether junior high camp should start at one or two in the afternoon.

One annual conference kept only the standing committees and put the chairperson of other committees on the CCOM without a committee. Those chairpersons draw up a task force as needed. Both laypersons and pastors can serve on only one conference committee. District superintendents need to avoid committee meetings like the plague. District superintendents are needed, day after day, to meet with the pastors and to visit in the churches. Why? Ministry is performed by local churches. That is where disciple-making occurs.

Ineffective ministers will have to be weeded out, using leave of absence, disability leave, and administrative location. Churches do not exist to serve ministers. No pastor can be permitted to destroy half a dozen churches as he or she flounders in personal confusion or professional ineptitude. No longer should a pastor be guaranteed a job for life. It is not good enough to send a grossly ineffective pastor to the "boondocks." The small church deserves a "workman who needeth not to be ashamed." A seminary degree is not a work permit.

The local churches can ask where the action is and can organize accordingly. *The Discipline* allows some freedom: One huge church recently organized an administrative council with task forces, tightening the structure to form tasks that the people were really excited about. It is not unusual to find growing churches that bend a few of the organizational rules in order to have time to get at the Lord's work. It is better to have ten people calling in homes than to have a "paper" commission on evangelism.

Nationally, because our church is smaller, we can no longer afford the luxury of vast boards and a honeycomb of committees. We used to argue that we needed big committees so we could put minorities, persons with handicapping conditions, women, and age group representatives on them. We wanted to be democratic, inclusive, and representative. The quota system was necessary to force us out of a white male syndrome of power.

It costs one hundred thousand dollars for some of the

general boards to meet. I would trust a woman from Montana, a youth from Chicago, or a black pastor from Atlanta to decide the policies of those boards and agencies. Currently, we don't have money for missionaries. We don't have money for new churches. We are fat where we should be lean, and lean where we should be fat. Something is wrong with a church that has larger boards of directors than it has staff for those boards. Something is askew with a church with more administrative staff than missionaries. We need inclusiveness; we don't need a huge bureaucracy.

As soon as possible, the whole church, including all committees, cabinets, and all administrators, should be watchdogs for total inclusiveness so that special committees to insure inclusiveness of race and age and persons with handicapping conditions can be superseded by mission to the world. We need everybody to help; let's mobilize our structures, not so much to be empowered as to empower the movement.

The System

I asked Lyle Schaller to comment on United Methodist structures. He listed twelve penetrating observations:

1. Currently "the system" rewards numerical decline and punishes growth. (Who receives the subsidies?)

2. The system encourages pastorates of two to five years rather than long pastorates. Longer pastorates stimulate growth.

3. The graduates of some seminaries are more likely to be pastors of numerically growing churches than are the graduates of other seminaries, but this is not a factor in advising people on which seminary to attend.

4. The first priority is to take care of pastors; taking care of churches is a lower priority.

5. Big congregations account for a disproportionately large share of new members received every year, but the number of large congregations has shrunk by one-third since the 1968 EUB/Methodist merger.

6. The capability to be pastor of a numerically growing

61

church is not a factor in admitting ministers to conference membership.

7. The compensation system rewards pastors who leave the pastorate for a denominational position rather than rewarding ministers who remain in the pastorate. (Exceptions do exist.)

8. The new church development process now requires a series of permission-giving steps that discourage new church development.

9. Motion pictures are the most effective channel of communication to move a congregation from decline to growth, but the UMC chooses to emphasize the printed word and slides to change attitudes.

10. The women's organization (United Methodist Women and its antecedents) once was organized around principles that were inclusionary and now is organized around exclusionary principles.

11. The organizing principles advocated for youth ministries tend to result, ten years later, in those youth not being active members of any church, or at least not in a United Methodist congregation.

12. In a world that offers people choices, the UMC tends to offer two choices—take it or leave it—rather than three or four positive choices.

Schaller concluded: "I expect, Bishop, that you may find that the present United Methodist Church *value system* will make it impossible to change most of the present operational policies that appear to inhibit numerical growth. That may place your committee in the position of advising pastors and congregations who want to see their congregation reach, serve, and include more people to ignore much of the present UMC value system and many of the current operational policies. Examples of that can already be seen in dozens of large congregations now experiencing numerical growth."

The Leaders

In any organization, leadership is a key. A congregation does not go far without a pastor with "gifts and graces." A strong layperson in the right place can turn a church around. Strong cabinets, dedicated to the task before them, can change the climate.

We have concluded our bicentennial, a celebration of famous people. Peter Cartwright fought with his fists to bring men and women to God. Martin Boehm preached in a barn on Pentecost Sunday. Philip Otterbein heard the message, embraced Cartwright, and exclaimed *Wir sind Bruder.* Francis Asbury refused to marry so that he could ride, ride, ride with the message of salvation.

Leaders focus the attention of everyone in the organization on the issues that are important. Leaders remind the people what the collective goals are. In our world on the brink of nuclear war, we can make disciples who will join us as peacemakers. In our society of injustice, we can make disciples of all races and, by our strange mixture, cause the world to see a sign of the kingdom. On a spinning planet where children bloat from famine, what an opportunity to draw people to Jesus, who fed the multitude and brought children into his arms. In a guilt-ridden age, what a time to help folks experience peace at the foot of the cross. It is time to reach out again. Leadership can make it happen.

The task of leadership is to center in on that which is vital. A writer in the field of business says that the institutional leader is primarily an expert in the promotion and protection of values. For example, Walter Hoving of Tiffany's said, "We must be true to our own aesthetic," and Tom Watson of IBM reminds the company that they believe in "respect for the individual." The Caterpillar Company takes pride in its slogan, "Forty-eight-hour parts service, anywhere in the world." Can we again speak of the work of Christ in the human heart?

> Jesus! the name that charms our fears,
> That bids our sorrows cease,
> 'Tis music in the sinners' ears,
> 'Tis life, and health, and peace.
> ("O For a Thousand Tongues to Sing")

It will not be easy to refocus the church's attention. Trends, like horses, are easier to ride in the direction they are going. A freight train, traveling sixty miles an hour, applying full brakes, takes one full mile to stop, and in so doing, ruins all the braking wheels. Our church has been on a long-term downward spiral. Powerful voices have shouted out from time to time, but the warnings have been unheeded.

Leadership at all levels of the church can change the emphasis. Societies, like individuals, can only handle so many concerns. A person can keep only so many problems and concerns in his or her head and heart at any one time. Organizational experts agree that if you want to move a company or some other kind of institution in a new direction, people within that institution must share a sense of that direction." The book *In Search of Excellence* discusses this theme of leadership. Leaders "pay attention to some things and not to others. Their actions express their priorities."

Leaders of our church must be concerned about the least, the last, the lost, and the lonely. We will not be doing the work of Christ if we do not invite the sinsick, the confused, the sorrowing, and the guilt ridden into our community of faith and share with them the message of the work of Christ in the human heart. The times call for decisive and dramatic leadership. Someone must mind the store.

UP FROM THE
ASHES

On January 2, 1974, as I drove across the frozen Kansas wheat fields toward Wichita, I was one scared preacher. My bishop told the Pastor Parish Committee that I was assigned for three years. He said they couldn't fire me until I had a fair chance.

The church had been in serious decline for eleven years, going downhill like a bobsled—just like the denomination—only faster. It was not because of its leadership; it had been served by some of the finest pastor-preachers in the United States. It was not because of its building; people came from all over the United States to see the magnificent contemporary sanctuary built in 1961 by Wagner of Philadelphia and Benedict of Wichita. It was not because the city was defunct; Wichita was a haven of prosperity, with a growing population of nearly 300,000.

Yet, in those eleven years, membership had dropped from 3,875 to 2,300—down 40 percent. Attendance in worship had fallen from 1,300 to 800—down 40 percent. Church school attendance had declined from 1,000 to 500—slashed in half like a furniture store close-out sale. The children's department was dismal, down from 600 to 200. The chairperson of the Pastor-Parish Relations Committee looked me right in the eye and said, "Dick, 60

65

percent of our congregation is over sixty years of age. It's your job to build a new congregation beneath us."

Most downtown Protestant churches in America were in trouble at that time. Over half of all such city churches had already been closed since 1945, half of the remaining will be closed before the end of the century. New neighborhood congregations had been culling the young families out of the old First Church. When visitors came, they commented on the sea of elderly faces in the worship services. We were burying between forty and fifty saints a year. There was a faint rustling of shrouds.

I paint this picture in dark hues to indicate that we were ready to grasp at straws, to read our Bibles, to say our prayers, to study church growth movements—to do almost anything to reverse the trend. As a congregation, we faced what our denomination is experiencing today; old First Church was a microcosm of The United Methodist Church.

Turning Evangelism Inside Out

I knew we had to develop "church growth eyes." Some folks weren't interested, just as many people in The United Methodist Church today do not care about reaching the unchurched. One top layman said he was interested in quality, not quantity. But I've never been overly impressed by the quality of wilting flowers. In fact, in the Acts of the Apostles, we find the finest hour of church life reported in the Bible. It was when people would do almost anything for one another and for the Lord that the church experienced its most dramatic period of growth.

Some people said we shouldn't prostitute ourselves by trying to grow. I agreed then and believe now that we don't need a membership drive. Our goal is not to be successful in terms of size or salaries or sanctuaries. Nor do we want to be spiritual scalp hunters, preoccupied with statistics. But if we're not interested in people and their spiritual needs, we might as well close up shop. Our Lord commanded us, as we were going into the world, to make disciples. His own ministry was a call to discipleship. He said the kingdom of God is like a mustard seed that grows until the birds fill its branches. The great banquet feast is open to everyone, and they shall come from the east and the west and the north and the south. So we, in that congregation, began to work just as our great denomination must go to work today. But, like Thomas Edison, we invented a lot of light bulbs that didn't work. Some of our plans for evangelism went bump in the night.

Take a quick look at our tragic trail of failures.

Stumblings

First we tried *pastoral calling*. There were several of us on the staff. I figured that if we worked hard enough and long enough, if we beat the bushes, we could grow. It had worked for me in the 1960s. Then I could set appointments at 6:30 P.M., 7:30 P.M., 8:30 P.M., and 9:30 P.M. in suburbia, and I would receive one or two families the following Sunday. Incidentally, in those years, 1957–60, The Methodist Church had over 1,500,000 membership transactions a year; that is, people going on and off the church rolls. We only had 950,000 in 1983. One reason we're in the mess we're in today is because many of those transactions in the late fifties and early sixties were superficial. Pastors could get people to sign a membership card on Thursday, receive them on Sunday, and lose them in the next few months. Experienced pastors today don't want to go down that trail again.

Besides, pastors who call on total strangers "cold turkey" find little success in the city. It may still work in the village or small town, but in metropolitan USA when a preacher calls on strangers, funny things happen. People aren't home. He or she can't get in the apartment complex. A man drinking a beer while watching television calls to his wife, "Reverend who?" It's hard to get an appointment. The unchurched often couldn't care less. I used to ask, "Are your children in Sunday school?" They'd say, "Gosh, our kids ought to be in Sunday school." Now they say, "No, they aren't." In the early sixties I used to ask, "Do you folks have a church home?" And they'd say, "Gee, we ought to have a church home." Now they say, "A what?" We wore ourselves out and got nowhere. We were wasting our time. Later, we had a layperson telephone all visitors within twenty-four hours to talk to them about our church program. It was much more effective.

Then we tried *two by two evangelism*. For years I had trained laypersons to go calling in teams. We would enlist forty persons to give four nights. They would make four calls a night—six hundred forty calls. We'd call on everybody. We brought people into the church. But today, in the city, for a layperson to take a handful of cards and go calling is discouraging. Once again, people aren't home; they're working the second or third shifts. Women often will refuse to let strangers into their apartments or homes. Church growth leaders are right when they speak of "relational evangelism." Today you have to build rapport before you can make any progress.

Now it was time to get desperate. We looked at *Evangelism Explosion*, James Kennedy's plan of hanging sinners over the flames of a burning hell. It's difficult for me and for most United Methodists to ask a perfect stranger, "If you died tonight, would you go to heaven?" It seems abrupt, rude. I think that sometime, somewhere, somebody ought to ask that question, but I don't have the stomach for it in a first encounter with a stranger.

Next we joined the *I Found It* campaign. In the city, a hundred churches trained a thousand telephone volunteers to call every number in the greater metropolitan telephone directory. The effort was to lead people to Christ over the telephone. We, ourselves, trained fifty telephone volunteers and made five thousand phone calls. Our only result was to have two or three people to promise to come to church—they never did—and one alcoholic who belonged to a different denomination promised to talk to his pastor.

Finally we tried a *mass rally*. We wanted to have a Billy Graham campaign, but our city was not large enough, so we had Leighton Ford in a great crusade involving several congregations. We invested twenty thousand dollars and a year's worth of energy in preparations. It was a marvelous time of ecumenical worship, of singing with the Nazarenes, the Baptists, and the Assembly of God folks. The hall was filled, and the gospel was proclaimed with vigor and wholeness. Some of our folks rededicated their lives to Christ. But nobody new joined our church; our decline continued.

Hints of a Breakthrough

Then, as if in spite of ourselves, we watched some interesting developments occur. It was as if evangelism had turned itself inside out. People who weren't even members began participating in programs of the church. I began to meet some people in the corridors who were taking an active part in the life of the church, and I didn't even know them. They weren't members. They had been attracted to the fellowship, and were as yet uncounted as far as a faith commitment and a church commitment were concerned. We had been operating under the model of Acts 2:40, trying to win people to Christ, then to receive them into the church, and then to assimilate them. Isn't that what we've been taught?

A New Model

Now, we began to experience a different model—Acts 2:42, 46-47. Laypersons invited newcomers to their church school classes, the choir, the youth program, the Bible studies, and a few were coming, taking part and learning what church was all about. Soon it began to happen that as I gave the invitation on Sunday morning, one or two people would come out of the choir, or out of an active relationship in a church school class, now ready to join the church. They first came, got involved, made friends, and then were drawn to a commitment. *They were assimilated before they were received. They were a part of us before they were converted.* Several became active in their classes or sang in the choir for six months before they were baptized and joined the church.

I remember reading, years ago, the book *New Life in the Church*, which emphasizes the need for a gracious community. The author, Bob Raines, quotes a German theologian who said, "In Luther's day, people were looking for a gracious God. Today, people are looking for a gracious neighbor." To put it another way, following the anti-institutionalism of the sixties and taking seriously the suspicion of sophisticated urban America, people want to know that religion is real before they are ready to believe. Some don't know enough about Jesus to accept him. Others have been "burned" enough times that they are wary. The wonderful thing about the new experience was that the people were not fly-by-night; they were with us.

One day I talked with a pastor of a rapidly growing suburban church. I asked about evangelism. He said he believed in the "mudball" theory. He went on to explain that when a boy makes mudballs and throws them at a fence, some of them stick and some of them fall off. That's the way he looked at church growth. He invited everybody he could to join his church; some of them stuck and some of them didn't. He said that about a third of them stuck, and then he added, that's about as good as anybody does. I was shaken, both by his candor and by the awful reality of what he was saying. What a far cry from the careful, spiritual supervision given the early Methodists in the class meetings. What a cheap way of treating the vows: "I will be loyal to The United Methodist Church and uphold it with my prayers, my presence, my gifts, and my service." What a frightening loss of members who will one day be taken off the rolls by church conference action.

Now in our congregation we began to examine carefully our ports of entry. To what groups were these new people attracted? It was the opposite of what I would have supposed. Was it to our strong, well-established adult school classes? No. It was to our new young, feeble, struggling adult classes. Was it to our United Methodist Women, one of the strongest in the nation? No. Only women who were already strong Christians, generally United Methodists, and generally over fifty, joined there. Younger women and newcomers came to a prayer fellowship and to a young women's share group. Our best evangelists were not our old faithfuls; their friends were already in the church. Our evangelists were newer, more insecure people in newly formed groups who still had friends in the outside world. Their Christian experience was so fresh that they were telling others about it. Their feeling of acceptance in the Christian community was so exciting to them that they wanted others to share it. So we began aggressively developing new ways of entering fellowship.

Adult Classes

The adult Sunday school was our first target. Established classes had lived so much life together that they were invisibly closed to the fragile, timid newcomers. It's difficult to put new wine into old wineskins. A new class was open, receptive, unsure of itself, and vulnerable. Newcomers felt more comfortable. We tried to start a new class about every six months. Some of them died aborning. I still can't believe it takes nearly two years to get the "infant" out of danger. We had a great deal to learn. Starting new classes is hard work and takes much time. We were helped by the book *Strengthening the Adult Sunday School Class*, by Dick Murray of Perkins School of Theology.

Now whenever anyone would come to our church his or her name would be brought to our attention, and we invited that person to one of the classes. We didn't talk about joining the church. That would come later, after we had eaten together, prayed together, studied together, laughed together, and played together. The church school grew from five hundred on Sunday morning slowly across a ten-year period to one thousand on Sunday morning; of that number, seven hundred were adults. Eight classes became twenty classes. Acts 2:46-47 was recurring: "Day

71

after day they met as a group . . . and they had their meals together in their homes . . . praising God. . . . And every day the Lord added to their group those who were being saved."

Single Adults

In Wichita, we took a special look at single adults. In America, 40 percent of all adults are single—unmarried, divorced, or widowed. Why has our denomination been so slow in recognizing these people and their unique needs? Our congregation sent observers to the Crystal Cathedral in Garden Grove, California, to Tenth Street Baptist Church in Houston, to Lover's Lane and Highland Park United Methodist Churches in Dallas, to the evangelical world of singles to see what was going on. Singles in the city often lead lives of quiet desperation. I have seen men whose wives have left them, taking the children with them to some far-off place, speak a word of pain in an adult class. I have watched as half a dozen people walked over and put their arms around that man. One man, who later became a leader in that singles' group, shared one morning what it meant to sit in his apartment and drink alone, without a friend in the world. He then looked around at the group and softly said, "I don't know where I'd be if it weren't for all of you."

I asked the bishop to send us an associate minister. We had a special requirement: she or he had to have been divorced. The bishop said that that was the first time a request like that had come. The Reverend Doug Morphis is now beginning to share with the whole nation ways that a congregation can have an umbrella of ministries to the single community. Also, now it's becoming clear that the minister does not need to be single. A minister of singles can be married and have eleven children, if he or she will give serious attention to the various needs of single people and help them establish a program, a fellowship, and a ministry that meet the deep spiritual, social, and intellectual needs of the members.

72

Young Adults

There's another upside down thing that happened. Wichita housed thirty thousand students. We thought surely we could have a college class. We tried for three years on Sunday morning, but to no avail. Then one day I asked the young man who was working with our youth ministries if he could come to a meeting on Thursday night. He said no, that's when his Bible study group met in his apartment.

"Who comes?" I asked.

He answered, "Oh, some of the kids from the university."

I pursued, "How many come?"

"Oh," he said, "about twenty or twenty-five."

"What do you do?" I asked.

"Oh, we study the Scriptures, drink pop, and talk," he answered. "We study the Bible. That's okay, isn't it?"

I answered, "The Bible is approved United Methodist curriculum. When do you quit?"

"Oh," he said, "I have to drive them out at about eleven o'clock."

"Why won't they come on Sunday morning to Sunday school?"

He said, "Don't you know college kids stay up at night? They don't like to get up early on Sunday morning. Besides, they don't want a lecture. They want to talk. They are on a serious spiritual quest."

When I thought of the hours our Commission on Education had spent trying to develop a college class and of the teachers who had tried so hard, I looked at this young man in blue jeans and tennis shoes, who had a vital fellowship in his crowded livingroom, and shook my head in amazement. They were meeting in a home, breaking bread, and praying, just as in New Testament times.

Later, some of those students started coming on Sunday mornings, teaching in the church school, forming a college and career class, and sitting on the front row in worship. Three of them now are studying for the ministry.

Women

Now consider the women. Our United Methodist Women, in their desperation, asked how in the world would we draw young women into the church. One of their leaders came up with a brilliant idea. She said, "Let's ask some of the younger women what they would like to have." Seemingly, no one had ever thought of that before. I hadn't. They polled twenty or thirty young mothers in the church and in the community and got a fascinating response. They didn't want to meet at noon or in the afternoon like the United Methodist Women. They wanted to meet in the mornings and desperately needed a nursery, because they didn't have anyone to take care of their children. They didn't want to meet monthly; they wanted to meet weekly. They didn't want to meet in their homes because they were too small, and there was no place for the children. No, they wanted to go to the church every Thursday morning at about 10:30. They didn't want a program; they wanted to share and ask questions of one another. They didn't want someone to give devotions; they wanted to pray, pray for their needs. They didn't want an educational program; they could get that on television. They wanted to ask one another questions of real importance, like: "How do you keep your sanity when your baby cries all day?" or "Does God really answer prayer when your friend's baby is dying of cancer?" or "How can we hold our marriages together when all of our friends are getting divorces?"

I peeked in one day and saw forty women holding hands in prayer. On another day I listened as a young woman, mother of two, wife of a traveling salesman, looked tearfully at the woman beside her and said, "A few weeks ago I was ready to take my life, and I think I would have if I had not been invited to come to this group."

The effort cost the UMW thousands of dollars in nursery costs until the group became self-sufficient, and those young women never really understood the UMW program, but they experienced healing and faith. They were drawn into the fellowship of the church.

Youth

In the late sixties, the youth program was almost nonexistent. A bored handful of youth wandered downtown for the traditional Sunday evening UMYF. A former pastor wisely held listening events throughout the congregation. He learned that the people desired to have an active youth ministry in the church. So, after a search for leadership, two young people were found, both in their early twenties. They intended to go at it a bit differently. Instead of trying to have a youth choir to sing on occasion, they met on Wednesday evenings for a couple of hours to study the Bible, pray together, and sing. Then they began to sing every Sunday morning at the early service, and the group sometimes sang for the sick and the elderly. They wanted to be called, "The Free."

I knew it wouldn't work. They were trying to put the junior and senior high classes together. They didn't have much musical training. No one would come all the way downtown on Wednesday evening for practice and fellowship. Even our adult choir only practiced for an hour and a half. The kids wouldn't want to study the Bible and pray—they wanted hot dogs and popcorn and ping pong—I thought.

One night they invited me to pray with them before an evening concert. I thought they would want me to give a perfunctory prayer. Instead, when I entered the chapel, I found them already in prayer. I sat down and listened as individuals offered brief but moving prayers. One girl, kneeling at the prayer rail, began to pray for her sister who was in the state reformatory. I looked around and saw young people I had never seen before. Where did they come from? Later I asked the youth sponsors about the girl. They said she had come a few weeks before because of a friend and was taking the whole thing very seriously. I was not surprised a few months later when she called to make an appointment to talk with me about being baptized and joining the church. She said, "I have found such love and friendship in this church. My family has fallen apart. Here is my *love* home."

We learned that young people need some forms of their own; that contemporary music is a great vehicle for youth; and that they are not afraid to work. In fact, they respond to a challenge. They want to be fed the meat of the gospel and to chew on it. Kids join the fellowship before they know who Jesus is; as they find out more about him, they are drawn to him and his church.

I've been away from that church a long time now, but I was not surprised to learn that they have eighty to ninety youths on Sunday morning, singing great anthems that are both contemporary and classical; these young people have led many of their parents and other young people into the life of the church.

We just received a letter from our daughter, Susan, who once sang in "The Free." She serves as director of youth ministries at McFarlin United Methodist Church in Norman, Oklahoma. Susan is getting the message. She writes:

Dear Dad, here is a youth program at McFarlin Church that is important and exciting. It is called the McFarlin Youth Intensive Care Unit. The name, intensive care unit, is chosen because it directly defines the purpose and desire of the program—to provide intensive care by youth for youth. As you know, a hospital intensive care unit provides personal care. Its purpose is to monitor patients meticulously. It requires the skills and talents of many. The unit must be prepared to respond in an emergency. It is a life support system.

At UMYF each Sunday night we have intensive care units. Each unit is made up of six to nine youth and a sponsor. For the last ten minutes of each meeting, we divide into these units to care for one another. The unit's responsibilities are to keep attendance and watch for any problems that may arise with one of its members. It is to be caring and action-oriented. The group follows up on absences with phone calls and cards. They send cards when someone is sick or in a crisis. Each member has the opportunity to share individual joys and anxieties. They pray together. The units require the skills and talents of all the members. All are emotionally, mentally and spiritually involved in each others' lives. It is non-stop care. It is a vital life support system to the youth program.

When we began the intensive care units, we were all admitted to the "unit" by filling in our admission papers, which requested our phone numbers, free times during the week, and our personal and spiritual needs. We all received a hospital I.D. bracelet and a listing of all the members of our unit and their telephone numbers to be carried in our billfolds. We are praying for one another, learning about one another, and finally, learning how to care for one another like Christ cares for us.

Music

Everyone remembers the popular song, "I Never Promised You a Rose Garden." Do you remember the book by the same title which inspired the song? The book, by Hannah Green, tells about a severely schizophrenic young woman named Deborah. The story burned a hole in my brain. Here's why:

As Deborah was improving in her intensive psychotherapy, and after she had been released from the hospital, she sang in a Methodist choir. But she left, disillusioned:

> She would know the Methodist liturgical year . . . but she would never penetrate an inch under the politely closed faces whose motions she duplicated. Over the text of John Stainer's "Sevenfold Amen," she looked out into the congregation on Sunday and wondered if they ever thanked God . . . for friends . . for friends . . . for friends.
>
> That evening at the church, Deborah invited her hymn-book mate out for a soda. The girl blanched and stammered. . . . Slipping back into invisibility, Deborah sang on through choir practice about compassion.
>
> In this town, though I sing beside them—they don't see me. They will never see me.

Deborah left the choir saying to herself, "I spent my hope singing with you . . . and when I stand next to you, you don't remember who I am."

The director of music ministries at First United Methodist Church in Wichita helped us understand that a choir is not a music-making instrument; it is a vehicle for bringing people into Christian fellowship and experience. Most churches expect the saints to sing. This director's philosophy was to ask everyone to sing—nonmembers, new members, visitors—she asked them to sing in the choir. People came on Wednesday before they came on Sunday. Imagine the thrill of having people come down out of the choir, already knowing folks in the congregation, already part of a life of prayer, study, and interpersonal relationships, now ready to make a commitment to the Lord and to the church. The chancel choir, itself, now triple its original size, had powerful spiritual dynamics. The scriptural texts were studied to explain their meanings. People who were sick or in trouble were remembered in prayer. The choir was divided into groups of four who were responsible for looking after one another in a special way. A late Sunday night Bible study and special lenten spiritual studies were normative. These people became tithers and people of prayer. In short, the director wanted the choir to be a port of entry for the Lord and the church, and she made it that way. People met Christ in the choir, and that doesn't always happen.

Analysis

Now, looking back, let me try to analyze what seemed to happen to us over these nearly eleven years. Bishop Mortimer Arias was a great help to me in this analysis, for he was once chair of evangelism for the World Council of Churches, and he sees disciple-making from a Third World perspective.

Koinonia

The word *koinonia* means to "hold in common." The Corinthians shared in the sufferings of Paul *(koinonia)*. In the letter to the Hebrews, Christians "share the reproach" *(koinonia)*. The bread which we break is a participation *(koinonia)* in the body of Christ. *Koinonia* is that mysterious form of Christian fellowship in which we hold in common the sacrifice of Christ for us, the mystery of being a part of his body, and the common task of working with God to save the world.

The United Methodists are a happy, positive, loving people. The society we live in is desperately hungry for our kind of acceptance, affirmation, and communal joy. It is a sin for us to withhold this experience from the isolated people of the world. If our church is to be reborn, it must experience once again the life of the early church: "They spent their time in learning from the apostles, taking part in the [*koinonia*], and sharing in the fellowship meals and the prayers" (Acts 2:42).

Centripetal

Mortimer Arias distinguishes between centrifugal forces and centripetal forces in evangelism. Some missionary work and some evangelistic work must be centrifugal. That is, it is radiating outward, divergent, deviating from the center like a ball on a string; that's the way David's slingshot worked. The genius of centrifugal evanglism is its outward thrust. Much missionary work, especially the planting of new churches is, at first, centrifugal. But today, with people so fractured, so fragmented by life, the spiritual need is often the opposite. People are disoriented or, as we say, "going off in all directions." The need now is to pull in toward a center.

Centripetal witnessing means to invite people into the fellowship and to help them grow toward the center or axis, which is in fact Christ himself; we are talking about inverted evangelism, witnessing turned inside out. Instead of inviting people to accept Christ, then join the church, then become a part of the body life of the church, the strategy is 180 degrees in the opposite direction. Bring people into the corporate life; that is, toward the center.

Let them experience the joy, the music, the Scriptures, the prayers, the love of the people. As they sing "Amazing Grace," they may find it. As a person experiences the acceptance of the fellowship, he or she may find the love that will not let go. Then, in the *koinonia*, as the people grow closer to the axis, their lives will become integrated, whole, and in harmony with God, neighbor, and themselves. This integration is the healing of the self in its triangular form that is the self with God, the self with neighbor, and the self within.

This inverted evangelism has a Wesleyan heritage. We preachers tend to idolize the Wesleys and George Whitefield for their preaching; indeed, they were centrifugal and did go out into the open fields where the people were. But historians tell us that more conversions took place in class meetings than ever occurred under the preaching of those noted evangelists. They stirred people up with their preaching, but then invited them to come to the group meetings. When Wesley was preaching, he would invite people to join a class, and would sometimes form a new class that very evening. He would explain that the one condition for class membership was simply "the desire to flee the wrath to come, know the acceptance of God, and live a higher life."

An entourage of workers traveled with Wesley. During the open-air services, they scattered among the crowd, studying the faces, conversing with the people, and inviting them to join a class. The salient objective in much of the field preaching was the starting of classes. These gatherings illustrate the centripetal force of the Wesleyan revival. The spiritual power of the youth program was not in reaching out, but in drawing in. The growth of our choir came by pulling men and women toward the center, not by getting on a horse and riding off in all directions.

Hospitality

Church growth experts are teaching us that many churches are not hospitable. They have no outdoor signs, or else the signs they have are in disrepair. The front door is locked, and only the "insiders" know how to get into the church. There are no ramps or elevators for persons with handicapping conditions. Although the formal "whites only" signs are not posted, the atmosphere of racial exclusiveness often pervades. The yellow pages in the phone book do not carry the time of service; ushers do not make the visitor welcome. Many of our churches are uninviting to newcomers.

More than this, the United Methodists no longer open their homes. The most powerful hidden resource for our church in winning new people to faith and fellowship is our homes. We have become so acculturated to our sophisticated American society that we want our homes to be places of privacy and refuge. We resent any intrusion. If we opened up 10 percent of the homes of United Methodist people for one night a week of Bible study and prayer and invited newcomers into the fellowship, it would revolutionize the church.

In New Testament times, Mortimer Arias reminds us, hospitality was a distinctive mark of Christians and Christian communities. "Open your homes to strangers" (Romans 12:13b), says Paul in writing to the Christians in Rome. "Welcome one another as Christ welcomed you." In Paul's description of the traits of the leaders of the church, hospitality is paramount. In the letter to the Hebrews, Paul raises hospitality to the rank of a very privileged duty: "Remember to welcome the strangers in your homes. There were some who did that and welcomed angels without knowing it" (Hebrews 13:2). And finally, Peter makes hospitality the right thing for all Christians to do: "Open your homes to each other without complaining" (I Peter 4:9).

Notice that this hospitality includes both those we know—our brothers and sisters in the church—and those we don't know, "the strangers." Spanish and Latin Americans have carried out this tradition, which is encased in the common expression, *mi casa es su casa* ("my home is your home"). Why is it that hospitality became so

81

strong in the New Testament portrait of Christians? The secret is already in the Gospels; the guest (the neighbor, the stranger, the least of these) is a sacrament, a token of the very presence of the Lord, himself. *I was a stranger and you took me in. If you have done it to the least one of these, you have done it to me. Whoever welcomes you, welcomes me and the one who sent me.*

Historians of the church have pointed to the fact that one powerful element in the extension of Christianity during the first centuries A.D. was the practice of hospitality. There was a huge network of pilgrims, Christian homes, letters, and traveling friends, which gave Christians in the Roman Empire a unique experience of fellowship, communion, and mutual support. During the Middle Ages, convents and monasteries became centers of hospitality, where the Christian faith was not only taught and shared, but also lived, demonstrated, and incarnated in hospitality.

Think of the power of hospitality for witnessing and disciple-making! People will come to our homes who will never, at first, come to our churches. People with less education, or more; with less money, or more; of lower social status, or higher; or of different racial backgrounds will come to our homes if we invite them. They will drink coffee with us before they will drink communion wine with us.

Missionaries around the world know this. Their homes have often been centers of Christian love amid hostile and unreceptive settings. If we think about it, some of us may owe much of our faith development to hospitable homes of pastors, teachers, friends, or strangers with a Christian heart and hearth.

An Assembly of God preacher moved to one of our midwestern cities about six years ago. His church of fifty members was in a trailer park in a low rent part of town. Today the church has six hundred worshipers on Sunday morning. When I interviewed this pastor, I asked him how in the world had he built up this great congregation. He said that his congregation was just old-fashioned "Methodists." They just had their lay people invite folks into their homes one evening each week. I went on to ask what was done in the meetings. He said that they studied the Bible and talked about problems people have, or problems in the community or the world, and that they prayed for one another. He said that the people invited folks who lived in the trailers next to them, or their acquaintances at work, or friends at school. When asked how many groups the fellowship had, he responded, "We've started a group every few weeks. I guess we have about fifty or sixty groups now that meet in the homes. Each one has about eight, ten, twelve, or fourteen persons in it. That is about all the houses will hold." Then he said, "Of course, I teach the leaders one night a week, just like Wesley did." I thought to myself: That preacher is a closet Methodist. Everyone in his groups has fellowship and spiritual nurturing. The leaders are being trained and held accountable. The church is making disciples.

That Assembly of God preacher didn't need committees. He didn't need a high-powered bureaucracy. He didn't even need a bishop. All he needed was some lay people who were willing to share their faith and their homes with others, and who were willing to be taught, guided, and held accountable by their pastor.

Raise your hand if you love Jesus is not good enough. *Sign this commitment card and join our church* rings of superficiality. Today, most people behave as though they come from Missouri—they say "show me" before they believe something is real. So let's invite them into the fellowship and draw them toward the axis. Let's create new *koinonia* units capable of welcoming the stranger. In the gatherings, let them read the Scriptures, pray for one another, eat at the table, and experience the community of faith (see Acts 2:42). As they are welcomed, they may touch the hem of the garment of Christ and be healed.

When people taste the flavor of the fellowship, eat the bread of hospitality, share the songs of Zion, study the historic word of faith, they will be pulled toward the center. Standing in that center will be Jesus Christ, who, if he is lifted up, will draw all men and women to himself.

CHAPTER

V

ATTACKING THE TWENTY-FIRST CENTURY

The twenty-first century belongs to lay Christians and to preachers who know how to teach them. In the decades ahead, the minister's task will be critical, not because ministers must run faster or do more, but because they will be called upon to inspire, to convert, to train, and to build the community as never before.

Clericalism, the notion that the preacher does the religious work, is as dead as last year's bird's nest. Just as Roman Catholic clericalism in the Middle Ages meant priests read from the Latin Bible, said the mass, and ran the cathedral, so United Methodist clericalism in the twentieth century involves preaching, pastoral care, church administration, and running madly about looking for lost sheep. Clericalism is kaput.

An Urban World

The *National Geographic* recently printed pictures of the gigantic cities of the world. In centerfold style, urban sprawl was depicted as a mass of humanity. Netza, Mexico's new exploding metropolis near Mexico City, comprises 2.3 million people in mile after mile of crowded housing. Demographers calculate that the earth held approximately one billion people in the early nineteenth century; two billion in 1930, and four billion in 1975. By 1999, they estimate a total of six billion; by 2025 (within the life expectancy of most people under forty) there will be eight billion people on the earth!

Picture in your mind's eye urban sprawl—American cities like Houston and Miami, Chicago and Minneapolis-St. Paul, Los Angeles and Phoenix—and contemplate the church's task. Ask yourself: If I were sent to one of these cities, how in the world would I go about winning people to Christ and the Church?"

Methodists and EUBs were effective in rural America, both in frontier days with a circuit rider and class leaders, and later with a resident pastor and a vibrant Sunday school. Around the turn of the century, when 90 percent of our population lived on the farm, a pastor of the "little brown church in the vale" could call on neighbors, invite them to church, preach to them on Sunday, and visit the sick and dying. The pastor even had time left over to study the Word of God and plant a spring garden. Some preachers are still trying that form of ministry all across America. Many lay people, suckled on the same style, are encouraging them to do it, even if it means nervous collapse on one hand or ineffectiveness on the other.

The church of tomorrow will look back at Wesley's strategies, gaze long and hard at the city, and take a fresh approach. The preacher/trainer will reclaim his or her Wesleyan rights as a change agent for God and go at it urban style.

Have you wondered why Billy Graham has called The United Methodist Church our country's greatest hope for evangelization in the future? Have you pondered why Robert Schuller dubbed The United Methodist Church a "sleeping giant?" It could be because there is a United Methodist Church almost everywhere in the country. Or it could be that we have a great organizational structure capable of approaching the people of our nation with a concerted strategy. But I think the reason is different. I think these two men—Graham and Schuller—who have dedicated their lives to evangelism, each in his own way, have in mind a Wesleyan history and heritage that is a reservoir of power standing behind us. We must simply choose to draw upon it. Our future will spring from our past. Our hope is in our heritage. We must be who we are called to be, and we are Wesleyans. Apart from that, we are nothing.

Now, what does this mean?

A Biblical People

The people who win the hearts and minds of countless millions in the next century will be a biblical people. If we are to claim the future, we will be "people of the Book." As United Methodists, we have always seen ourselves as standing in the mainstream of salvation history. The covenant made with Abraham, Isaac, Jacob, and Joseph is our covenant. The commandments given through Moses are our commandments, as we view them through the mind of Christ. The ringing cry of the prophets Amos, Hosea, Jeremiah, and Ezekiel are shouted to us and through us. The psalms are our songs of faith. The Christ who entered history as the revelation of the being and grace of God is our Christ, our Savior, and our Lord. His new covenant is our covenant: "You who once were far off have been brought near in the blood of Christ" (Ephesians 2:13). We are a Gentile people grafted into the tree of faith (see Romans 11:17-24).

The church that carries the day in the years ahead will not be a disjointed religious group, not a "people's church," not a bunch of cultists who rewrite their own philosophies. It will be a church of Jesus Christ marching to the historic messages of Scripture.

We are not fundamentalists, not literalists, not inerrancy addicts. Wesley wasn't; neither are we. Oh, there was a time when Wesley opened the Bible and put his finger down at random for inspiration, but he quickly gave that up. The word *inerrancy* is not a biblical word. The Southern Baptists will stub their toes on it, and it will cause grave dissention. Our problem is a different one. We have taken so seriously scientific analysis of the Scriptures, using higher and lower criticism, historical and contextual understanding, that we have often forgotten to hear what God is trying to say to us. While we do not take the Bible literally, we must take it seriously. It is the sufficient rule both of faith and of practice. As Kierkegaard suggested, it is the whispers of God in his marvelous "love letter" to us. Through the words of Scripture we can experience the *Word*. We listen to God speak to us as we read, pray, and think within the Scriptures. Without the authority of the Bible, we have no authority at all.

Of late, John Wesley's quadrilateral has been misunderstood. Many are now suggesting that there are four bases for Methodist authority: Scripture, reason, tradition and experience. The *quadrilateral* concept is used to support almost every heresy and pet theological opinion. Our foremost Wesleyan scholars agree that we are watering down Wesley's understanding. "Wesley's view," says Dr. Albert Outler, "goes like this:

Scripture is our authority, fundamental and decisive. The quadrilateral is not a geometric metaphor, as if the square had four sides, all equal.

Rather, Scripture is normative.

Tradition is the collective wisdom of the church in interpreting Scripture.

Reason is the critical discipline used in judging the credibility of all interpretation.

Experience is to the person what tradition is to the whole Christian community. Tradition, reason, experience are ways of understanding and interpreting Scripture.

But Scripture is central and normative."

Those who want to rewrite the Bible using their current philosophical or sociological perspectives do us a great disservice. If the God of the Bible is not able to lead us to wholeness and justice and freedom, then we are indeed lost. Too many people have spent too many years painstakingly poring over too many manuscripts guided by too much Holy Spirit for us to tinker with the texts now.

I have never seen people so hungry to know and understand the Bible as they are today. Across the country, in little towns and in cities, groups are gathered with their Bibles wide open to read, talk, discuss, and pray. The numerous translations, now often in colloquial versions, make the study immediately available to every person. But our spiritual ears must be open. We are not merely meditating on manuscripts by Paul or Ezekiel. We are listening with the ear of faith to the Word of God. A church that treats the Bible as a dead text will be like the Samaritan priests in Israel who display ancient manuscripts to the tourists. Every revival of faith has come about through a rediscovery of the voice of the Spirit in the Scriptures. Luther was studying Romans when the weight of fear and guilt was lifted from his soul. Wesley was listening to Luther's commentary on Romans in which Paul was describing the change that God works in the human heart, and Wesley knew that his sins were forgiven. Karl Barth, with German idealism crashing at his feet, rediscovered his Bible and forged a fresh foundation for faith in the midst of hatred and holocaust.

The Bible is our book, and we will carry it into the future with us. We will teach it to our people, and they will in turn teach it to others. Pastors must multiply themselves by training others; they must become preacher/trainers. The text for the future will be II Timothy 2:1-2: "As for you, my son, be strong through the grace that is ours in union with Christ Jesus. Take the teachings that you heard me proclaim in the presence of many witnesses, and entrust them to reliable people, who will be able to teach others also." Two helpful tools now available for teaching the laity are the Bethel Bible series and the Trinity Bible Plan. Other plans for training lay teacher/disciplers need to be prepared quickly.

A friend of mine, pastor of a large metropolitan church, shared with me with some chagrin this insightful personal experience. When he was pastor of First United Methodist Church in Dallas, he decided to have Lenten Bible studies in the homes. He taught a class, and so did his associate pastor. Because he was the senior minister, the pastor's home was filled to capacity the first night. The associate's was about half filled. Week after week, however, like the disciples of John the Baptist, the pastor's group diminished. The associate pastor's study group grew each week. Discouraged and somewhat disappointed, my friend asked his associate what he was doing wrong. He had gone to his seminary notes and was discussing the authorship, the design of the book, and the historical context, and he thought people would be very much interested in "studying the Bible." The associate said in response, "Oh, we're just reading the Scriptures and asking what God is saying to us that would be helpful in our daily lives." The difference in approach is the difference between listening for God's present voice and engaging in an academic exercise. One has spiritual power; the other has intellectual curiosity.

Ministers must do background research just as a surgeon studies new surgical methods, but when a person is lying on the operating table, he or she doesn't want a discussion on different styles of sutures; he wants to know if he is going to live or die. People today are hungry to know God, his saving grace, his moral imperatives, and his guidelines for everyday living. The seminaries of the future that equip men and women to serve a congregation must teach them how to help the laity become leaders in the biblical and spiritual nurturing of others. The first sign of a growing church is one with a strong emphasis on Bible preaching and teaching.

A Covenant People

In our society, people move about in isolation; in the church we never have to "stand it alone." In the fellowship "we are often troubled, but not crushed; sometimes in doubt, but never in despair; there are many enemies, but we are never without a friend" (II Corinthians 4:8-9). The urban world teems with aloneness. People drown in unattached emptiness. In the 1960s, the Beatles caught both the beat and the mood of our society. When they sang "Eleanor Rigby," they diagnosed an agonizing loneliness in our society. They pleaded with us to look at all the lonely people. They wondered where all the lonely people came from and where they all belonged. When the Beatles sang of this lonely isolation, they touched a responsive chord in millions of hearts.

The Wesleyan movement has always been communal in nature. Both John and Charles Wesley made their theology and administration an effort to help people grow within Christian fellowship. Not only are we a part of the historic covenant made first with Abraham and made anew in Jesus Christ, but we are also a part of a covenant community. Wesley said that there is no such thing as solitary religion. We have gone through the heresies of American individualism. Our emphasis has been vertical—"accept Christ and be saved"—as if there were no church, no covenant, no supportive community. One great heresy of the electronic evangelists is that they stimulate this individualistic interpretation of faith.

Two dramatic events occurred in early Methodism that inspired Wesley and will aid us as we march into the future. The first pivotal experience took place in the parsonage at Epworth. When Samuel Wesley went to London, Susanna stayed at home and saw to the need of teaching the Scriptures, first to her children, then to the servants, and then to friends in the church. They would gather in the parsonage to pray and sing. Susanna read and interpreted some of Samuel's old sermons to them. Such action was not authorized by bishop, priest, or tradition. Women were forbidden to exercise any spiritual authority or priestly functions. But it revitalized Epworth parish. Susanna defended her actions by writing: "It is plain, in fact, that this one thing has brought more people to church than ever anything did in so short a time. We used not to have above twenty or twenty-five at evening service, whereas we have now between two and three hundred, which are more than ever came before. . . ."

Severely reprimanded by the curate and then by her husband, she responded with great intensity that there was spiritual hunger, an ignorance of the Word, and the loneliness to be a part of the people of God. She wrote back to Samuel:

> If you do, after all, think fit to dissolve this assembly, do not tell me that you desire me to do it, for that will not satisfy my conscience; but send me your positive command, in such full and express terms as may absolve me from all guilt and punishment, for neglecting this opportunity of doing good, when you and I shall appear before the great and awful tribunal of our Lord Jesus Christ.
>
> *Susanna: Mother of the Wesleys*

Susanna's home fellowship was linked to the historic Anglo-Catholic community, it was grounded in Scripture and prayer, and it included people of all walks of life in the warmth of interpersonal faith friendships. Susanna made history. She planted a seed from which grew the Methodist concepts of a church within a church.

The second experience was a strange one, pointing to the providence of God. When the New Room—the first Methodist chapel—was built in Bristol it carried a significant debt. How to pay it off? Captain Foy suggested that if eleven Methodists met with him every week, he would obtain a penny from each of them or provide it himself. At first Foy intended to go around to see each one. That proved impractical, so they came together each week. That class met weekly for prayer and study and to pay off the debt. Wesley sensed the power in this gathering, power to hold people accountable for their spiritual growth, power to keep individuals from drifting back into secular isolation, power to provide emerging leadership among the Methodists. Wesley wrote: "They immediately joined them together, took account of their names, advised them to watch over each other and met these catechumens, that they might instruct, rebuke, exhort, and pray with them, and for them."

Wesley believed the Methodists were different from

other revival movements, for they balanced conversion and nurturing. Preaching conversion without offering nurture is like giving birth to a baby but not nursing it. Unnurtured converts are prey to the devil.

How many people can you love at any one time? Some psychologists say about twelve; that is, to be personally concerned, dedicated enough to help, willing to make regular inquiry, and eager to pray for each one daily, about twelve is all anyone can handle. No pastor can pray hard enough, run fast enough, or love deeply enough to hold hundreds of people in significant Christian fellowship by his or her own efforts. In the church of the future, the pastor will be training lay leaders, class leaders, and spiritual leaders who in turn will have ministries to all kinds of covenant groups in the life of the church. It will be the only way to penetrate the urban sprawl.

When Dr. William Hinson was appointed to The First Methodist Church in Houston, Texas, a church of thirteen or fourteen thousand members, he immediately began to meet with twenty-five key men at seven o'clock every Thursday morning, and with twenty-five key women at two-thirty in the afternoon. Almost all of these persons are under forty years of age. Dr. Hinson discipled these people. He taught them. They talked about what it means to be a Christian in a large city. They talked about Christian stewardship. They prayed. They studied the Bible. They talked about family life and about the pressures of our society. Sometimes someone would say, "I don't know whether I'm really a Christian or not," So they talked about that. Someone else would ask for prayer in a business or a family matter. Together they deepened their spiritual lives. Then, Dr. Hinson began to use these people in places of key leadership everywhere in the life of the church. They became lay ministers in training. Last year those key people were so energized that they provided 10 percent of the budget support in that great church.

Another model is the Church of the Servant in Oklahoma city. Dr. Norman Neaves, the pastor, helps the laity understand their ministry, and he puts them to work.

When persons become members of the church, they begin to find their places of spiritual service. Training is provided. Laypeople call on the shut-ins and work with the youth. Laypeople are in training for the Sunday schools and in how to call on the sick in the hospital. Lay people are leading discipling groups that meet in the homes and are forming new adult classes. On any given Sunday morning, about two thousand people are in study and in worship. They are a part of the community of faith. Pastor Neaves' job is to make sure that they are spiritually fed on Sunday morning. He and his staff of lay and clerical professionals see to it that the training programs are continual and comprehensive, and that every new inquirer is brought into the community of faith in such a way that he or she may be able to make a life-changing commitment and continue to grow in the fellowship. Emphasis is on covenant, community, training and ministry.

One of the largest Methodist churches in the world is in Seoul, South Korea. The pastor is both medical doctor and minister, Reverend Sundo Kim of the Kwane Lin Methodist Church. On Sunday, ninety-five hundred people attend one of the four worship services: 8:00 A.M., 10:00 A.M., 12:00 noon, and 2:00 P.M. Each weekday morning at 5:30 A.M., hundreds of the faithful gather for prayer before going to work. Every Friday evening, the forty-five-hundred-seat sanctuary is packed for a service of prayer and praise.

How do they provide those urban throngs a sense of community? The secret is the "cell"—the modern Korean Methodist class meeting. The congregation is composed of 1120 cells that meet for an hour or so at various times and places throughout the week. The cell is the dynamo providing power for the vast and growing parish. It is where people are converted and nurtured.

Dr. Paul Y. Cho, whose Full Gospel Central Church in Seoul numbered more than three hundred fifty thousand in 1983, has written several books describing the strategies used. In *More Than Numbers*, he explains the "cell" plan. Here are key points:

"I have learned how to use my lay people in the work of the ministry.

"I have over 18,000 cell leaders, both men and women.

"The cell leaders are carefully trained, motivated, recognized and complimented.

"The cell group is the basic part of our church. Great numbers of women leaders are used, a revolutionary idea among conservative Korean Christians."

A cell has a clear goal—the salvation of two souls each year. Potential converts are invited to a meeting at a non-threatening place with people they can feel comfortable with. For every thirty cells there is a licensed minister to pastor the people. The cells are clustered into twelve districts with each district headed up by an ordained minister.

Each cell has an assistant cell leader in training to break away as soon as the group is too large. At that time, he or she will keep in constant contact with the original cell leader as well as with supervising licensed ministers.

Imagine hundreds of thousands of people, motivated to reach out, yet being sustained in corporate life and watched over, every one, by a dedicated and trained cell leader. They come to celebrate worship on Sundays, not as isolated individuals, but as part of a covenant community. They are better cared for spiritually than many Christians are in a church of six hundred members where the pastor tries to nurture everyone personally.

Our church must put its best minds to work enabling preacher/trainers to make disciples. Then it must help those disciples to become lay ministers and class leaders, teaching them just as Jesus taught the twelve. Our pastors must experiment and innovate; our creative writers must help us with materials; our seminaries must train ministers who can multiply leaders.

Out of these powerful cells of community, all rooted in faith, all sorts of fruit will be harvested—social service, social witness, care for one another, compassion for others, and conversion of the lost. The flower of our Wesleyan faith will be firmly rooted in rich soil once again.

Passionate Pastors

The bishops express concern. The preachers are not enthusiastic; many are burned out, tired, overburdened. Some have succumbed to professional numbness and are wearily walking out the remainder of their careers. Some are philosophically out of gas.

Many are lonely, isolated by a laity that does not understand and is removed from a power structure it fears. A few have been wounded by life. Instead of being "wounded healers," they are simply hurting.

The distinguished author and pastor Maxie Dunnam wrote, "I think the heart of this problem really is in the clergy. I don't know whether we have been worn out or worn down, but wherever I go, I get the feeling that there is not the spark there should be. There is a lifelessness. We may be good 'professionally,' but we don't have a vocational drive to reform the continent and spread scriptural holiness across the land."

Many bishops agree. One former president of the Council of Bishops speaks of an "armor of complacency" owing to "very secure job security." Another former council president refers to the "shelters of a tenure system" that protects some pastors from accountability. Many church leaders agree that the parish minister is experiencing a "faith crisis." They speak in clichés like "low vitality," "little enthusiasm," "low priority on preaching, conversion, reaching new people," "much weariness," and "burnout."

The overriding opinion held by laypeople and pastors alike is that the local church will thrive when the minister is enthusiastic, and it will founder when the minister is dry and lifeless.

How can we energize our preachers for the challenge of the century before us?

Focus: Jesus Christ

First, we focus on Jesus. He is the magnet that draws men and women to God. Apart from him, the Word becomes word. In him, the Word becomes flesh. He is the center of the center. He fuels our faith.

Many theologies want to discuss God, but they make him an oblong blur. Jesus Christ is the content. He incarnates the character of God. His Holy Spirit is at work in the world through his word and through his body the church.

Preachers should burn, not burn out. They should shout, "I live; yet not I, but Christ lives within me!"

All the world has been intrigued and inspired by Mother Teresa, the Yugoslavian born nun who serves as "mother" to the poorest of poor in Calcutta, India. A *New York Times Magazine* writer once wrote that he is a non-believer, and is vaguely uncomfortable among people affirming their faith . . . yet, he spent two hours watching the small woman at prayer, sensing that in her communion lies the source of strength and the heart of her achievements. After all, she has several times made her point by saying, "I am not a social worker. I do it for Jesus."

So, too, we do our ministry for Jesus. He has laid claim on our lives. We are called not to be successful, but to be faithful to him. His Word and his Spirit refresh us. Because Jesus is the Lord of history, the church that moves with power and vigor in the complex years ahead will be his church. We need to emphasize his work; it will lift the burdens from our pastoral shoulders.

Focus: Sin

Part of Christ's earthly ministry was to reveal our human brokenness. His teachings focused on our self preoccupation. His healings often were forms of forgiveness. His cross showed what our sins cost God. If we are to be true to him, and true to our Wesleyan heritage, we will again be overcome with a sense of lostness. Once again, because we believe in a Savior, we will believe in sin.

Dr. Karl Menninger, world renowned psychiatrist, in his book *Whatever Became of Sin*, a decade ago tried to draw us back to our biblical moorings. He wrote,

The very word "sin," which seems to have disappeared, was a proud word. It was once a strong word, an ominous and serious word. It described a central point in every civilized human being's life plan and life style. But the word went away. It has almost disappeared—the word, along with the notion. Why? Doesn't anyone sin anymore? Doesn't anyone believe in sin?

The churches that are drawing people to them believe in sin, hell, and death. Jesus, who knew what he was talking about, explained them, experienced them, and conquered them. If there is no sin, we do not need a Savior. If we do not need a Savior, we do not need preachers.

No need for cheap sin—we've gone through moralisms, acting as if sin were a cluster of sins, like smoking a cigarette behind the barn. No, loneliness is too existential for that. Hopelessness is too pervasive for that. Loss of meaning is too personal for that. Nearness to death is too profound for that. We are broken inside. We are estranged from our neighbor. We are at enmity with God.

A husband and wife came to me once for counsel. He blurted out, "I don't believe in hell." But after he and his wife explained their adulteries, their angers, their jealousies, and their hurts, I said, "You don't have to believe in hell; you are experiencing it." He nodded in agreement.

A church that understands "lostness" will more likely understand "salvation." We point to Jesus because he shall save his people from their sins.

We did not go into the ministry to keep the public morals by lecturing folks on what they ought to do. We became ministers because we serve a risen Savior, and we point to him and his cross.

We United Methodists are rediscovering the cross, but the struggle is difficult for us. We have been turned off by "blood-of-Christ" preachers who isolate the cross from our Lord's total self-emptying of himself in his full ministry. We have been offended by the "price paid to the devil" or by "he paid it all" as if we have no responsibilities. But we *were* bought with a price. While we were yet sinners, Christ *did* die for us. Even if he or she stutters, the preacher has passion when saying, "I knew that my sins, even mine, were forgiven."

We have so much going for us—the Holy Communion, which never lets us forget the bread that was broken and the cup that was poured out; our precious hymnody which reminds us of the "Sacred Head Now Wounded"—but a part of our renewal depends on our willingness to teach and preach the saving work that Christ even now can accomplish in the human heart.

Focus:
Ministerial Training

Our seminaries, as they refocus on the scriptural foundation of our Wesleyan emphasis, must recapture both the depth of our lostness and the power of our Savior. It's too bad, in a way, that our theologies were not devastated by the wars, by the holocaust, and by the recent depravities of history. Our American optimisms still cover over our brokenness, like 200,000 dollar homes cover up family problems. Our idealisms still gloss over our awful despair.

Seminaries must fuel the faith of our new ministers. If they are only graduate schools, their graduates will be able to write term papers, but not to save souls. Too many seminarians continue on in doctoral studies not because they want to become teachers, but because they are hooked on books. Some wag has said that students enter seminary inspired to be evangelists and graduate aspiring to be seminary professors.

Signs of hope include a theological vibrancy brought on by a wave of second-career seminarians, for now the average age of seminary students is about thirty-five years. These new seminarians, both women and men, bring maturity, Christian experience, and existential questions to the classrooms. Chairs of evangelism, strengthened posts for preaching, Wesleyan emphasis studies, and serious internships are signs of bringing renewed sensitivity to human pain and renewal. Another hopeful sign is the marvelous number of women being called into ministry. They bring gifts and graces that enrich, spiritually and emotionally, the full life of the church.

Forty percent of our students do not attend United Methodist seminaries, some for economic reasons and others for theological reasons. That can be both good and bad. It is good if it keeps an ecumenical spirit within us, bad if it creates division. It's good for sometimes providing a stronger biblical emphasis, bad for sometimes being presumptuous, "holier than thou," or neo-Calvinist. It's good for sometimes giving emphasis to the Holy Spirit, bad if it's too pentecostal to work within our denomination. That is why Jesus Christ must be central to our recovery. If we are one in him, we will be one with each other.

Another hopeful sign in the seminaries is the interest in spiritual formation. Students are participating in various covenant and prayer/study experiences. We are not navel gazing; we are power gaining.

If we are to tackle the world for Christ, the seminaries must be fiery furnaces. The task is not to grant degrees, but to inflame the minds and hearts of a generation of preachers. Boards of Ordained Ministries will have to phrase their questions differently, or we will continue to quench the fires. Now the emphasis seems to be on jumping through professional hoops. We need to ask, of course, "Have you taken United Methodist polity?" but we also need to ask students to tell us about Christ's work in their lives. We must not only ask, "What is your view on infant baptism?" but also, "How are you equipped to lead men and women, boys and girls to God?"

Remember, Wesley had these four ordination standards for clergy:

a) Do they know God?
b) Have they received gifts?
c) Have they the graces?
d) Have they produced fruit? Are any truly convinced of sin and converted to God by their preaching?

Affirmation

The bishops and the cabinets, and in fact the laity, can build up the fires of enthusiasm by their systems of affirmation. What gets the applause?

Do we reward a minister for building up the church school? For teaching in the vacation Bible school? For sitting around a campfire at junior high camp, talking about Jesus the Lord? For working for a year with the confirmation class? For training twenty gifted laypersons to be teachers and spiritual nurturers?

In industry, cheers go up immediately when a victory is won. Tom Watson, president of IBM, believed in immediate rewards. One day, an IBM worker gave him a good idea; Mr. Watson looked quickly for something to give to him in return. In his drawer was the banana he had brought for lunch. He grabbed it, raved about the idea, and handed the man his banana. Instant affirmation. Now, IBM has instituted for giving a pat on the back the Top Banana Award.

In previous days, ministers were affirmed when someone was converted. In the black church, preachers would tell of their conversions and their new members at annual conference, and people would clap, praise God, and affirm one another.

Now, we seem content to ask preachers if they have "paid out" on their apportionments. Affirmation seems limited to getting a bigger, and presumably better, appointment. If our "jollies" come from financial gain, we best quit preaching and go into business. If our satisfactions come from larger churches, we will spend our ministries climbing a ladder that has no top—and most climbers will become disillusioned because most United Methodist churches are small.

But if leadership praises and rewards pastors for evangelism and education in the parish, vibrant growth will occur. More important, if a minister hears a testimony from someone who has experienced divine forgiveness, communal acceptance, or creative ministry through his or her efforts, that will be strong affirmation indeed.

Jesus sent out the seventy to witness, to preach the kingdom, and to heal the sick. They came back in great joy, and our Lord affirmed them, "I saw Satan fall like lightning from heaven. . . . But don't be glad because the evil spirits obey you; rather be glad because your names are written in heaven" (Luke 10:18, 20).

A pastor's ultimate assurance is the conviction that he or she is being used by Christ Jesus to do eternally significant work.

The Itinerancy

Our system is constantly changing. Once itinerancy meant single young men riding gallantly across the prairies. Later it meant moving every year or two, family, pets, and all, from one rural church to another with a "barrel of fifty-two sermons."

Now, as we face an urban world, itinerancy may mean not moving at all. Americans are mobile, especially in the cities. It used to be that the people stayed put and the preacher moved. Now the people move so the preacher can stay put.

Longer pastorates develop trust, stability, and confidence. Many a city pastor has noted his sixth, eighth, tenth, or fourteenth year to be the best. It takes two years for the people of the community to know you're there. It takes three or four years before inquirers will trust you. It requres six years to develop a significant leadership development program. Television and radio ministries slowly become more meaningful as the preacher becomes an old friend, like a clerical Johnny Carson. In a lonely world, a broken society, a trusted pastor who knows his people is a precious commodity.

Furthermore, many pastors are shell-shocked by their frequent moves. They and their families have been transplanted too often, like a tree uprooted too many times. There are no roots, no sustenance, no vitality.

On the frontier, people were bored and wanted new and exciting voices from time to time. Today, people are confused and lonely, overstimulated and bewildered. They want a familiar friend, a pastor they know, and a spiritual leader who can take them spiritually deeper than they have ever gone before. Lyle Schaller is correct in insisting that church growth is strengthened by longer pastorates. Churches with declining memberships often have short-tenured ministries.

Renewal

The fires must be stoked. Our ministers burn out if they are not continually encouraged and inspired.

Preaching can do it. Some annual conferences are swinging away from pure business meetings back to spiritual encouragement with singing, preaching, and time for fellowship.

Private devotional life can do it. Jesus, our model, was often alone in prayer. Pity that we preachers are not on our knees often enough. Father Henri Nouwen, in a lecture, once commented that our churches would be healthier if sometimes the church secretary would answer the telephone and say, "I'm sorry. Pastor is in prayer this morning."

Enriched family life can help. The ministerial family works under a tremendous amount of stress, as Dr. David Mace describes in his marvelous little book *The Clergy Couple*. What are we doing to help? Marriage Encounter, Marriage Encrichment, United Methodist Expression, and Celebration Marriage are powerful marriage growth experiences. Why are cabinets not modeling marital renewal by participating? Why are laity not offering to babysit and provide pulpit supply so their parsonage couple can attend?

The Emmaus retreat, springing out of the Cursillo movement, lifted me from heavy soul weariness a few years ago. As I rested, prayed, and received the Holy Communion from the hands of another, I heard the words in my heart: "Those who trust in the Lord for help will find their strength renewed. They will rise on wings like eagles; they will run and not get weary; they will walk and not grow weak" (Isaiah 40:31). I rose up refreshed, touched again by the living Spirit of Jesus Christ, and resumed my work.

It reminded me of the Ashram experience that revitalized my ministerial life when Julia and I, in a week's spiritual renewal, experienced the internal peace, the physical and emotional healing which the Holy Spirit brought to us.

Roman Catholics have much to teach us about spiritual renewal of the clergy. Some priests have a full-time ministry in providing renewal for the "religious" orders. Is there any place we can go, at any time, under any conditions, to be nourished and nurtured? Lectureships or Pastor's Weeks are often too academic or too frenetic with too little silence and too little prayer. If we are to be part of the healing of tomorrow's world, we must be healthy ourselves.

What about those ministers who hurt? Too often we move them to other churches, or encourage them to leave the ministry. Dr. Charles Swindoll claims that churches are the only outfit that shoots its wounded. Intense efforts toward healing the community, for personal and marital counseling, opportunities for rest and relaxation, appropriate leaves of absence or sabbaticals, and spiritual retreat and recreation renewal must undergird our future if our pastors are to be sustained in intensity.

The Professional Minister

Dr. James Glasse in the sixties wrote a book called *Profession: Minister*. Jim, a Presbyterian and my friend, meant well, but he took us in the wrong direction. He studied H. Richard Niebuhr's term *pastor/director*, but thought it did not go far enough. Niebuhr's term emphasized shepherding and guiding the community of faith; a good corrective to individualism. But Glasse emphasized competency, acquired skills, and professional status. The professional minister came across as a three-piece-suit clergyman who feels comfortable working side by side with a physician or an attorney or the president of a bank.

Dr. Glasse writes, "One becomes professional (1) by virtue of prolonged and specialized intellectual training and (2) the acquiring of a technique which (3) enables the practitioner to render a specialized service to those who receive it (4) for a fixed remuneration. Professionals (5) develop a sense of responsibility and (6) build up associations to test the competence and maintain the standards of conduct of the members."

I believe in competence. I believe in the skills of preaching, counseling, and administration. I believe in going to school. But the heartbeat of evangelical fire is elsewhere. Somehow the very word *clergy* smacks of smugness. Too much energy is expended for status. Too much attention is given to tenure, guaranteed appointments, and advancement to the level of one's peers. The men down at Joe's Auto Shop might speak with deference to Dr. So-and-so, but they would feel more comfortable talking with a preacher who acts like a human being who cares about them.

There are only two ways to evangelize, says Mortimer Arias: to *be* one of them, or to *become* one of them. The first is the farmer preacher, the class leader, the local pastor. In the Rio Grande Conference, churches served by these persons, that is, local pastors, are the ones that are growing. The importance of home-grown, often bi-vocational ministers cannot be overstated: The United Methodist Church cannot get along without them.

The other way is to evangelize cross-culturally. That requires a self-emptying rather than a self-affirming. The church growth experts, following Peter Wagner's lead, speak of E-1, E-2 and E-3. In E-1 we work with people of our own social status. It's the easiest and brings the most growth. E-2 crosses modest barriers of culture or social status; E-3 crosses severe barriers—national, racial, linguistic. The experts recommend E-1. But the gospel is most exciting and has its most dramatic impact when the "blood of Christ" (Ephesians) breaks down the barriers.

That requires *kenosis*, self-emptying. The model is Christ in Philippians 2:5-7: "The attitude you should have is one that Christ Jesus had. He always had the nature of God, but he did not think that by force he should try to become equal with God. Instead of this, of his own free will he gave up all he had, and took the nature of a servant."

As Wesleyans, we can attack the future with confidence, corporately grounded in his Word and fired by his Spirit. We advance Christ's cause, not to "grow a church," but to help heal a lost and hurting world.

VI

A TIME TO BURN

Janie, aged five, had twenty-seven cigarette burns on her arms and back when they brought her to the clinic. Her parents later said she was hysterical, and they couldn't get her to stop crying. Sammy, aged nine, was unconscious when the ambulance arrived at the emergency room. His mother said he had fallen down the stairs, but the doctors knew he had been beaten with a bat or club. Teeny, aged seven, had been sexually used by her stepfather for three years when she was discovered by Social Services. Both mother and daughter were afraid to say anything.

Child abuse is spreading like wildfire. Like wild animals ripping at a carcass, social forces tear our families apart. A family court judge once told me that he does little besides stamp divorce decrees—over sixty a week. It is difficult to keep up with movie stars and sports heroes who have marital breakups. We are close, in the United States, to having 50 percent of our marriages burning up and turning to ashes.

Domestic violence is epidemic. The General Board of Church and Society continues to be alarmed about pornography and violence. At one meeting, we viewed films that had been broadcast on open cable television. I thought they would be sexy. Instead, they were so sadistic, so violent as to cause grown men and women to close their eyes. Imagine a woman taking a bath in her home while a hooded man with a huge power drill bores through her doors and finally through her body. Such violent pornography is a multi-billion dollar business, and it often involves children!

The violence is not limited to the tube. A highway patrolman stops a car for speeding and has his head blown off by the driver. I made the pastoral call. An eighty-five year old woman a hundred yards from the church was robbed and then beaten to death by a young man who was angry because she had so little money. I conducted her funeral. A young mother in our congregation took a basket of laundry to the laundromat at 9:00 P.M. The sheriff discovered her body in a country creek the following morning. I identified the body on behalf of the family.

The world is on fire.

Persons are violated. In Boston, seven young men kidnapped a seventeen-year-old girl and raped her repeatedly for seven hours in an apartment belonging to one of the men. In Bedford, Massachusetts, four men raped and tormented a woman on a pool table in a local bar while onlookers cheered. At the University of Pennsylvania, members of a fraternity-gang raped a young woman at a fraternity party. The fires are burning everywhere.

It used to be that sports nuts like myself could read the sports page and find out how the games transpired. Now we read about the latest drug scandals, or the tense salary negotiations and strikes, or the under-the-table money given to amateur athletes. Greed, lust, and pride characterize the human condition.

We hold in our rich soil the silos of nuclear rockets, capable of turning this world into a burnt ball of smoldering ruins. Soviet Russia and other countries harbor the same weapons of doom. Our missiles are like wild stallions on a rope, straining to run wild. A nuclear war would make the holocaust of the 1940s look like a Boy Scout weiner roast. As Christopher Frye wrote in *The*

Lady's Not for Burning, "I've never seen a world so festering with damnation."

Paul understood it: "God has given those people over to do the filthy things their hearts desire" (Romans 1:24). The world is on fire. And into that world God has called his church, his holy people. In a world often burning with flames like those of hell, God has called his people to save it from death and destruction. When the church was born on the day of Pentecost, a passion for God swept over the believers, and a holy flame burned within them. It was a new kind of fire that put out the old. The fires of passion will destroy us. The fire of God can save us.

Look again at the sacred record recorded in the book of the Acts of the Apostles. All the believers were gathered together in one place. Then they saw what looked like a tongue of fire. No wonder Peter, when he stood up to preach, cried out in a loud voice the words of the prophet Joel:

> I will pour out my Spirit on everyone. Your sons and daughters will proclaim my message; your young men will see visions, and your old men will have dreams. Yes, even on my servants, both men and women, I will pour out my Spirit in those days, and they will proclaim my message. I will perform miracles in the sky above and wonders on the earth below. There will be blood, fire, and thick smoke; the sun will be darkened, and the moon will turn red as blood, before the great and glorious Day of the Lord comes. And then, whoever calls out to the Lord for help will be saved.
> (Acts 2:17-21)

We United Methodists need that fire again. The church was born in the fires of Pentecost. We were born again in the fires of the Wesleyan revival. T. S. Eliot was right, "We shall be consumed by fire or fire." We will be burned up by the fires of our own passions, or we will be energized by the passionate fire of God.

When the people of Christ are together and surrendered to our risen Lord, when we are of one mind and one heart and the fire of God's burning Spirit comes to us, then the church is born afresh and miraculous things begin to happen.

The Message and Language

When the apostles' hearts were strangely warmed, they began witnessing in different languages. The Acts experience is not a tongues episode like the Corinthian church had. The Jerusalem event was a missionary empowerment. Believers suddenly were talking about Jesus in different dialects and idioms. People could understand the gospel in their own languages. Communication occurred across ethnic, cultural, and linguistic barriers. There was a "meeting of meaning," to use Buber's phrase.

That's what happens when we ride on "chariots of fire." We can talk to the world in the languages the world understands. Right now The United Methodist Church does not speak many of the languages of the people of the world. I am not referring to French, German, Greek, and Spanish. Let me indicate some languages, some idioms in which we are mute.

Consider the poor. We do not speak their language very well anymore. Once we did, both in England and in the United States. Now we produce political pronouncements that focus on the plight of the poor; many of these pronouncements are helpful and appropriate. We engage in a compassionate ministry around the world, providing food, clothing, and emergency relief. But we are not including the poor in our fellowship. We do not seem to speak their language. Mother Teresa takes the poor in her arms. We are not doing that.

John Wesley started with the poor. He knew that the masses are generally more receptive than the classes. Wesley wrote:

> "I preached . . . at Haddington . . . to a very elegant congregation. But I expect little good will be done here, for we begin at the wrong end: religion must not go from the greatest to the least, or the power would appear to be of men." (Journal 5–21–1764)

Later, he noted that the fields were white for the harvest everywhere and said:

> There is everywhere an amazing willingness in the people to receive either instruction or exhortation. We find this temper now, even in many of the higher rank, several of whom cared for none of these things. But surely the time is coming for these also; for the scripture must be fulfilled, "They shall all know me, from the least even to the greatest." (*The Works*, XII, 192)

If our church school literature is too sophisticated, let us simplify it—or at least a part of it. If our churches are too verbal, let us have more opportunities for physical labor and social experiences. If our music is too classical, let us develop hymnals in which the music of the people can be sung again. Church historians will remind us that all creative and extensive periods of church growth have been characterized by an appropriate indigenous hymnody. One reason services of prayer and praise are so well received is that they are so human, so open to people of all educations and class. Do we have room in our church for pick-up trucks and blue jeans? Is there any place for country gospel music?

The new poor are the divorced women of America. Millions of mothers between the ages of twenty and forty are trying to raise their children alone. Month by month, untold numbers are slipping into the poverty category. What an opportunity for The United Methodist Church to minister with our day-care centers, our preschools, our children's nurture centers, our vacation church schools, our summer camps, if we care enough to include these people in our fellowship! What an opportunity for our singles ministries to reach out to the lonely, to the confused, and to the bewildered single parent families with the full supportive impact of the faith and fellowship of the church! God will give us the words to speak if we allow the Spirit to move within us.

I remember when Carol visited our worship service for

111

the first time. Her husband didn't care for church, so Carol walked the mile or so by herself. During the week, she made beds and cleaned at a nearby downtown motel. Her education was limited, but she loved music. At the close of the service, our director of music asked Carol what had brought her to our service, and she replied, "The music." The music director said, "Why don't you sing with us?" and Carol blushed. The director insisted, and the next Wednesday night, there Carol was. She had a pleasant voice and a glorious smile when she sang. Last Christmas I received a letter and a cassette tape from Carol. She wrote with pencil on tablet paper, "I wish you could have been here Christmas Sunday. It was a glorious service. We sang Handel. It was like being in heaven." I hope our church can speak the language of the poor—the language of love, affirmation, and acceptance.

Some of the poor are from ethnic minority groups. Many of the twenty-three million Hispanics in America are poor. Most of the Hispanics who join Anglo parishes are *yuppies*, second and third generation Hispanics who are moving up and out. Those who remain in the ghetto speak Spanish, often have little economic opportunity, and require a church of their own. In the last twenty years we have founded only eighteen or twenty Hispanic churches. Dr. Dan Bonner of First United Methodist Church in Brownsville, Texas, says we require a one-two punch. That is, we need to open up our congregations (as he has), and we must organize new congregations. But the question is: Is there room for minorities in The United Methodist Church?

My daughter, Sarah, is in the Peace Corps in Costa Rica. She spent the first three months learning to speak Spanish and is continuing to work on it so she can communicate with the people. Do we have people who are so on fire with the Holy Spirit that they can speak both Spanish and the language of the poor? Are we on fire to bring men and women to God and to bring them from marginal social existence into the mainstream of America?

Single Adults

We don't speak the language of the single person very well. Yet, 40 percent of all Americans are single, and the experts say the numbers will soon be 50 percent. Some have never married; some are divorced; and some are widowed. The language we speak often excludes the single adult. Church school classes are named "Double Ring," "Come Double," "Fifty-Fifty," or "Hand in Hand." For a divorced man or woman, that sounds like "no room in the inn." Family night suppers are often announced as if they were just for husbands and wives with two children, a station wagon, and a six-pack of soft drinks and a dog. Church growth experts argue that times of pain and transition are moments when people reach for God. The loneliness that pervades many a divorced person can be met by the fellowship of the church. The grief that depresses many a widow or widower can be assuaged by the understanding of the fellowship. The energies of many a not-yet-married person can be put to work in the creative tasks of the congregation. I find it intriguing that Jesus called Peter, a widower; Paul, a never-married; and Mary Magdalene, a promiscuous single, to be foundation stones for his church.

Exclusive language debilitates us. Instead of "family" night, we need "congregational" or "church family" night. Instead of family units, we need household units, so we can speak of the church as the family of God. When Jesus was interrupted by someone who said that his mother and brothers were there, he turned, looked at the multitude, and said, "Whoever does what my Father in heaven wants him to do is my brother, my sister, and my mother" (Matthew 12:50). Our Lord creates family, and if we are attuned to his Spirit, we will include those whose human family ties are broken. Large parishes should have personnel to work exclusively with these individuals.

Some congregations have divorce therapy groups. Others have grief healing fellowships. Some have

Thursday night singles' meetings or Tuesday evening Scripture studies for singles. Many a church school class has been formed, targeted for this population. All sorts of economic, social, emotional, and spiritual values are provided.

A minister's widow once came to my office, restrained but angry. She said, "Why doesn't the church care about people who have lost their mates by death?" I responded that we pastors call in the home. We conduct the funeral. The congregation provides the meal. What was she talking about? She answered, "That's just it. Three weeks after the funeral, we're forgotten. No one cares about our finances, about the laws that are restrictive for widows, about our ongoing grief, or about the estrangement we feel in our own churches." I asked what she proposed. She handed me a book she had been reading called *Where Have All the Flowers Gone?* It tells of fellowship groups formed to sustain men and women who have lost their spouses by death. Immediately we got a group of people together to talk about it. She volunteered to be a full-time unpaid worker. Soon there was a therapy or healing grief group announced for the city that would meet each Sunday afternoon for six weeks. Arrangements were made for a counselor to be available and referrals to be made. Special classes were taught on household finance, household repairs, and cooking for one. Then she organized W.H.O.—Widowed Helping Others. It was ecumenical, city-wide, and open to all. People came out of the woodwork. Over a hundred men and women assembled monthly for fellowship and special programs. Most of all, symbolically it said that somebody cares. Some of these people united with our church; others did not, but people felt the Spirit of God was at work.

Radio and Television

What is the universal language? It is not esperanto, but television. When we appear on television, we walk into thousands of bedrooms and sit down in countless livingrooms across the land. Scarcely any home is too poor, too rich, or too remote to have a television set. Everybody speaks the language of television.

Radio continues to be a powerful medium as well. Many a family wakes up to a clock radio. Almost every car has one. Lots of folks leave it on at work all day long.

The church in the twenty-first century will have to be vocal and visible in mass media. Television and radio do not take the place of the local church; that is the great weakness of the electronic evangelists. They have been entrepreneurs in this field because the mainline churches have been strangely silent. The secular world brings the passions of fear and lust into our homes in living color. The TV evangelists often bring a truncated gospel, sometimes prostituted by huckster gimmicks and usually estranged from a faithful congregation. Why are United Methodists not speaking the language of Christ's peace and love in the most powerful communication medium ever devised? Pioneers in the field, pastors like Bob Goodrich of Dallas Texas, Ed Bauman of Washington, D. C., D. L. Dykes of Shreveport, Louisiana, and Charles Allen of Houston, Texas understood this a quarter of a century ago. We can't penetrate the urban scene without speaking over the airwaves.

We have been hesitant. We have been stingy with our money. We have been afraid to allow some "superstars" to have visibility, preferring instead to try to keep everybody at the lowest common denominator. But just as Ralph Sockman's radio pulpit from New York City spoke to the nation in the name of Methodism for a quarter century, so we need voices speaking today on behalf of our entire movement. The "Protestant Hour" on radio could be much more powerful than it is if it had the cooperation of the churches in every town and city, and if it had a serious promotional strategy. The United Methodist Communications group is launching a program in 1986 called "Catch the Spirit." The programs are excellent. It has a certain "I'm proud to be a United Methodist" flavor and deserves wholehearted support.

115

The strongest voices in television are currently on a regional basis. People like Stephen Steward in Tarzana, California, Mouzon Biggs in Tulsa, Oklahoma, John Gatewood in Key Largo, Florida, Barry Bailey in Fort Worth, Texas, Bill Hinson in Houston, Texas, Richard Faris in Virginia Beach, Virginia, and a score of others across the land are well-known in their areas, and speak clearly and forcefully on various aspects of the gospel, right out of their own local churches.

I'm amazed at how few churches decide to use local radio and television programs in an effort to explain and interpret the gospel. Much of what we do is second- or third-rate quality, and so far, most of our material is limited to worship services. The world is waiting for the church to have children's programs, Christian education—material in the form of puppet shows and special talented teachers—helpful material on family life, and discussions of nuclear disarmament and racial justice. When the Spirit moves within us, we will talk to the world in the language the world understands. We will speak on talk shows, radio shows that feature Christian music, or an analysis of secular music, discussion of religions and ethical news, material on the Christian home, helps in living a single Christian lifestyle. Many a small-town radio station is open to creative programming, sometimes at no cost, sometimes sponsored by local merchants.

Of course, in the mass media, the Word of Christ goes smack dab into the secular world, but that's the world we are trying to penetrate. Once in our televised worship service we had a communion service that lasted a bit too long. As I passed the cup and said, "Drink ye all of this," we suddenly went off the air, and were immediately replaced by a burly truck driver who thrust out a mug of beer and said, "When you say Bud, you've said it all." That is the world we live in. We have to fight fire with fire. If we continue to be hesitant with the mass media, we will leave a vacuum to be filled by the independent evangelists and the parachurch groups. If their gospel appears partial or if their appeal seems to be self-serving, we really have no one to blame but ourselves.

For ten years the services at First United Methodist Church in Wichita have been broadcast on the CBS affiliate, KTVH, Channel 12, and boosted in Western Kansas so that the signal reached into parts of Colorado, Nebraska, and Oklahoma. The station estimates that the program reaches thirty-five to fifty thousand people each Sunday morning. What good does it do? It strengthens the elderly. It gives mainline Protestantism a voice for interpretation of current issues and the gospel. It causes many people to give the church a second look. It provides worship services for the sick, those in the hospital, and the shut-in. It gives visibility to the church, not just the church from which the signal emanated, but all United Methodist churches, so that we are like "a city set on a hill that cannot be hid." Bulletins are mailed each week to five hundred shut-ins statewide so they could follow the service. Some pastors take bulletins to the hospitals on Fridays or Saturdays and tell their people they can watch a United Methodist service. People of other denominations appreciate the good will, the ecumenical spirit. There's no question that for the church in urban America to be viable, in addition to intimacy and caring within the fellowship, it must speak the language that the world is hearing.

Ministry

Now when the fire of the Spirit burns within us, look what happens not only to our message, but also to our ministry.

There were professional priests in New Testament times, just as some of us are full-time pastors and priests in our time. But the Spirit empowered everyone who believed. The fire of God burned in each breast. "I will pour out my Spirit on all people," prophesied Joel, "and your sons and your daughters will prophesy." No sexism here. "Your young men will see visions, and your old men

117

will have dreams." No ageism here. Methodism began to burn like a prairie fire, and when the Wesleys couldn't handle the flames, they turned quickly to the laity. John Wesley, almost in spite of himself, had to say in effect, "Here, Harry, you carry on with the society in Bristol tomorrow night. And you, Susan, you be class leader of those twelve new converts at Lovely Lane. And you, Samuel, look after the widows in South London."

If the church is to burn today, the pastors must train the laity for ministry. Every layperson must be asked, "What are your talents, and what are your spiritual gifts?" Each pastor, like Wesley himself, must teach and train the laity for their spiritual ministries. As a national news magazine recently commented on the Roman Catholic church, "It is no longer pray, pay, and obey." In The United Methodist Church, it can no longer be serving on the finance committee, being a trustee, or fixing chicken for the bazaar supper. Those duties are important, but we now need Christian people who can speak the languages of the people. We need on-fire-faithful who will teach and make disciples, lead family life discussions in their homes, guide studies on peace in their church school classes, and invite young adults into their livingrooms for fellowship. We need people who will minister to the elderly in the nursing homes, read to the blind, visit the jails, and help kids get off drugs. We need the laity to hear confessions, offer prayers of forgiveness, and lead Bible studies. We have fires of passion to extinguish. God needs people who burn with his love to help put them out.

Many pastors, instead of trying to save the world all by themselves, are beginning to provide biblical and theological training to the lay people in their congregations, and they are finding it the most exciting part of their ministries. Recently, a doctoral study asked two hundred rural pastors of different denominations what gave them the most feeling of success. The one ingredient that emerged as a common theme was the success they experienced in teaching and training the laity.

Several experiments have brought this truth home to

118

me—both have Lutheran orientations. The St. Stephen Ministries is designed for caring and compassion. After a year's training, these laypeople are eager and capable in the nurturing of the ill, the elderly, the shut-in, and those troubled by divorce and grief. Some are working in hospice care; others provide special compassion for needy families. Often they work on a one-to-one basis. A good number of churches now have thirty or forty such persons working under the guidance of a lay coordinator. One St. Stephen's lay minister, a retired guidance counselor, is in charge of a one-to-one compassionate ministry with one hundred twenty shut-ins in her congregation. What a ministry of healing! What a beautiful spirit of caring in a bleak world!

Thousands of congregations across the United States, of a variety of denominations, are using the Bethel Bible study for biblical and theological grounding. This plan requires two years of study with the pastor and then offers those people as teachers for a congregational phase of Bible study.

I realized a few years ago that our church was caught up in busy work. At the same time, our active people, especially those under forty, could not understand simple biblical allusions in the sermons. New people were expressing an interest in Bible study. So, we sent several members to study the Bethel Bible Plan, and we took the leadership training program. I'll never forget returning to the church with the instruction from Bethel: Set aside the best evening of the week for study. In our church, the best evening was Wednesday when all of our commissions, committees, boards, and councils met. I remember sitting with my associate pastor and a key layperson, looking into one another's eyes and talking. Finally, one of us said, "It's time to put first things first. Housekeeping is second to spiritual formation. Bethel Bible goes on Wednesday; the committees have to meet on Monday." That act alone began a transforming action in the congregation, for soon, after training our leaders for two years, each Wednesday night three to four hundred people were studying the

Scriptures; not all were members of the church. The signal went up that housekeeping was necessary, but it was in second place. More important, laypeople were becoming scripturally literate. They were eager for more study. They were receptive to teaching classes, guiding home groups, and providing key leadership. They began to visualize themselves in ministry.

The Trinity Bible Plan, written by Frank Warden, a United Methodist pastor, although not designed specifically to train teachers for the Trinity Bible program, gives excellent grounding for those who will be teachers and leaders in the congregation. Pastors looking for a one-year training program should seriously consider the Trinity Plan.

If I were to again enter the parish ministry next Sunday morning, the first thing I would do would be to select twenty or thirty gifted laypersons and I would meet with them once a week to train them to be special spiritual leaders in the life of the church. The fire of the gospel will burn when the entire people of God is energized.

Mission

We have seen what happens to our message when the fire comes, for we will speak in many languages. We have seen what happens to our ministry, for the whole people of God will be put to work. Now, look what happens to our mission. We begin to burn. Someone once asked Robert Schuller how many ministers his church had. Dr. Schuller answered rather abruptly, that the questioner had just made three mistakes. First, it isn't his church; it belongs to Christ. Second, although the Crystal Cathedal has several clergy members on staff, every member of the congregation is a minister. Everybody who joins the Crystal Cathedral is in ministry. Only a few are clergy. And third, they are not a church; they are a mission station. Every congregation ought to be a mission station.

In *Megatrends*, John Naisbitt comments that the railroads were the most prestigious corporations in America.

The Pennsylvania railroad was chosen as the best run corporation in the world. This is not so today. Now, the railroads are in disrepair and disgrace. What happened? Naisbitt says those in charge of the railroads misunderstood the law of the situation. The law of the situation requires that we ask ourselves what business we are really in. The railroad magnates thought they were in the business of running railroads. Wrong! They were in the transportation business. What might have happened if they had understood they were in the transportation business? Naismith conjectures that Pennsylvania Railroad would have been expanded to include trucking, airlines, and would have seen its whole task as moving people and produce effectively and efficiently from one place to another.

Many people believe that our business is to run the church. That's why we're in trouble, just as the railroads are in trouble. Our job is not to run the church; our job is to save the world. "For God did not send his Son into the world to be its judge, but to be its Savior" (John 3:17). We need a new vision of mission. Oh, let us pray that our young men and young women will have visions of a world transformed, that our old men and old women will dream of a church on fire. Our job is to save the world, to take the whole Gospel of the whole person to the whole world.

John Wesley understood that we have to innovate and sometimes bend the rules if we are to burn for Christ. In 1772, Wesley wrote, "To this day, field preaching is a cross to me, but I know my commission and see no other way of 'preaching the gospel to every creature.'" Wesley was so intense. He said to his preachers, "It is not your business to preach so many times, and to take care of this or that society; but to save as many souls as you can; to bring as many sinners as you possibly can to repentance, and with all your power to build them up in that holiness without which they cannot see the Lord." That's why Wesley was so willing to innovate. Dr. Hildebrand reminds us in *Christianity According to the Wesleys* that evangelism can never be the field of specialists or the target of extraordinary years and seasons of Methodism. It must be the normal work of the whole church the whole time—unless the church ceases in truth and in deed to be the church of Christ.

Robert Schuller, speaking to the National Congress of United Methodist Men in 1985, called for a rebirth of mission. He said that very little doubt existed in his mind that The United Methodist Church today is a sleeping giant. Stirred into action, it could produce in our time the most sweeping spiritual, social, economic and political changes in the history of this world. The United Methodist Church has the theology and the organization to literally sweep this country for Jesus Christ. No other denomination has the power, the ability or the freedom to attract the masses of people as does The United Methodist Church; this giant has been lulled to sleep. If this church begins to flaunt what it has and this giant begins to wake up, watch out, for it could literally change this world for Christ.

I remember a young woman who was burning—burning up inside with guilt, loneliness, and sexual cravings. She is an illustration of our world aflame. I'll call her Jeanette. She walked into my study complaining that she was overeating and gaining weight, as if I were a diet counselor.

As we talked, she mentioned growing up in a small town, attending UMYF, going to the university, living with a fellow for a couple of years, preparing for a wedding that never happened. When the man walked out, she began to work hard, weep a lot, and eat. Dates were one night stands—in the sack and out.

As she talked, I thought of others I knew who were burning just like Jeanette. I thought of other counseling sessions that only touched the surface, of prayers I had offered that only bounced off the ceiling. "Dear God," I prayed, "if only the fire of the Spirit could be ignited within her so she could be at peace." But I needed help. I needed the apostolic word, the supportive community, the prayers of the faithful, the incisive skill of the Great Physician.

Then I remembered. On Wednesdays, a Christian psychologist came to our church to serve as a trained therapist for anyone in need. He served as a pastoral associate from a local community mental health center. Jeannette's psychosomatic symptoms cried out for this professional care.

I thought of our new young adult church school class that had grown out of a Thursday night group. I laughed inside myself, remembering the Board of Trustees meeting in which I asked to remodel an old building so the class could meet on Sunday mornings. One trustee, a banker, said, "Preacher, you want us to remodel the building we're going to tear down?" I said, "You bet. Remember, we're not a money saving institution; we're a people saving institution!" I have never felt the Holy Spirit more powerfully than when those trustees voted to carve a church school room out of a derelict building.

As Jeanette continued to talk, across my mind flashed the little prayer group of young women from that class, and of the young adults who sat together in worship. Suddenly I blurted out, "Jeanette, here's what I want you to do: I am going to make an appointment with our therapist. Will you see him?"

She said, "Yes."

"You need Christian friends who will treat you as a human being, not as a disposable object. Will you come to our young adult class?"

She nodded. "I'm going to have a fine young woman call and invite you to the prayer group. Okay? And come to worship if you can."

I never said much about Jesus. But the counselor called me and said that after several interviews he and Jeanette concluded their final session with prayer. He literally saw her straighten up her shoulders, dry her eyes, and beam with a new joy in her heart. Now when I saw her trim figure, she was laughing, surrounded by newfound friends.

Her mother wrote me a letter which proved to me that God is still alive. She wrote, "Jeanette has come 'home.'" She didn't mean back to her hometown, but *home* to God, *home* to her family relationships, *home* to her true self, *home* to the church. The fires of guilt, loneliness, and sexual cravings had been quenched. A new fire burned within her.

I thought Acts 2 was happening all over again. Many miracles and wonders were being done, and everyone was filled with awe day after day. They met as a group in the temple, and they had their meals together in their homes, eating with glad and humble hearts, praising God. And every day the Lord added to their number those who were being saved (see Acts 2:43-47).

The United Methodist Church can burn again with the fires of Pentecost. The Holy Spirit can empower us to speak in all the languages of the world, can enable all women and men, old and young, of every race and nation to be inviting witnesses of peace, and can inflame the mission of Jesus Christ to save a lost and lonely world. We will be consumed by fire or by fire.

* * * *

Comments and responses to the material in this book are welcome. Please address correspondence to Bishop Richard B. Wilke, c/o Abingdon Press, 201 Eighth Avenue South, Nashville, Tennessee 37202.